Meant to Be

By

James G. Verity

authorHOUSE™

1663 LIBERTY DRIVE, SUITE 200
BLOOMINGTON, INDIANA 47403
(800) 839-8640
WWW.AUTHORHOUSE.COM

First published by AuthorHouse 03/03/05

ISBN: 1-4208-2844-4 (sc)

Printed in the United States of America
Bloomington, Indiana

This book is printed on acid-free paper.

Forward

From the day I was born until present moment, a countless number of people – good, learned, holy people have been a part of my life. Each one of them exerted a profound, lasting influence on me. I wish it were possible to thank all those who helped me to be a better person.

For the very few who may have harmed me, I wish it were possible to tell them they are forgiven, that I hold no grudge. And by the same token, I wish it were possible to ask forgiveness of those I may have harmed.

Wouldn't it be wonderful if we could have a great big, joyous reunion with all those who have touched our lives and give each one of them a handshake, a hug, or a kiss of peace? Let's hope that God in some mysterious way can arrange such a reunion. This shouldn't be too difficult for the Almighty. After all, looking back over my life it is pretty obvious that He had a hand in many of the acquaintances I made.

And isn't it possible that with all the twists, turns and about faces we make in a lifetime that His guiding hand is always there not to push, shove, or force, but to nudge us gently in the right direction? We can be confused and even agonize over what path to follow, and yet regardless of how feeble our call might have been for guidance, God still listened.

A storm tossed sea captain recognizes when the lighthouse keeper calls him into a safe harbor. The captain could never thank the lighthouse keeper enough just for being there when he was most needed.

I don't believe that people walk in and out of our lives purposelessly. Nor do I believe that the events, planned and unplanned, which fashion our lives happen completely without rhyme or reason.

If we believe in an all knowing, provident, and merciful God, then my wife, Cecilia, has it right when she says, "It was meant to be."

Chapter One

In the early 1900s, Brooklyn, New York was called the City of Churches with good reason. The Bushwick section of Brooklyn was no exception. All one had to do was to climb up the nearest "El" station and look in any direction to see the steeples and the temples. Bushwick had its share of Protestants, Catholics and Jews. It was a working class community with a majority of German and Irish residents, a small percentage of Italians and a sprinkling of Jews.

Bushwick had little variation in its lifestyle or daily routine. Like clockwork, the men in early morning would be hastening to catch the trolley or Broadway "El" on the way to work. Basically, there were three types of workers: the clerical workers in their suits, high collared white shirts and ties; the uniformed cops and firemen; and the overalled tradesmen with their lunch boxes and tool bags. These men left their homes at a brisk pace in the morning and returned home, twelve or fifteen hours later, at a much slower pace.

Once the women got their men out of the kitchen and off to work, they were back at the stove cooking oatmeal or farina for their school age children. At about eight o'clock, the sidewalks were crowded with children carrying their school bags and lunch boxes. School buses were not needed; all schools, private and public, were within walking distance.

With the men and school children out of their way, the women could concentrate on their infants and toddlers, and the serious chores around the house. The water would be boiled. The washboard would come out and the scrubbing started. The washing cycle always hinged on good drying days. On a sunny morning, sheets, pillow cases, towels, shirts and underwear could be seen dangling from the clothes lines which stretched from the kitchen window in the rear to the pole in the backyard. Depending on the size of the family, the first batch of wash would be reeled in to be replaced by socks and stockings, diapers and knickers, and school clothes. There were few secrets in Bushwick. A quick look at the clothesline told you about the skills of the housewife, the employment of the husband, and the number and ages of the children.

When the work was done and the housework completed, it was time to bundle up the infants and dress the toddlers for the first daily trip outdoors. All neighborhood stores were within walking distance. The supper menu was determined not only by the budget and best bargains, but also by the amount of food that could be crammed into the shopping bags to be carried home. The number of mouths to feed determined the number of trips to the stores. All in all, shopping was exciting for the housewife because she could get out, meet her friendly neighbors and hear what was happening on the block. For the children, a trip to the bakery was always a favorite, especially if the jovial lady behind the counter gave them a free cookie. Second best for the boys, was the butcher shop where they could run and slide on the sawdust floors. And if the boys behaved while their mother selected her cuts of meat, they would be rewarded with a free slice of bologna. Wise butchers and bakers attracted the young mothers, not only with the quality of their products, but by the kind attention they paid to the young cherubs who accompanied their mothers.

By three o'clock, the mothers were back in the busiest room in the apartment – which was a combination of a kitchen, dining room and laundry. The kitchen table was the most active piece of furniture in the apartment. It was not only surrounded by hungry adults and children at meal times, but was also the largest open space for folding laundry, reading newspapers, and doing homework.

When the final school bell rang, the kids who walked slowly to school in the morning, came running down the streets in the afternoon. If nothing special happened in school, it was a quick, "Hi Mom," a fast inventory of the icebox, a rapid change into play clothes, and back into the street. The boys into the gutter, choosing up sides for stick ball or touch football. The girls sitting on the stoops or skipping rope on the sidewalks.

In late afternoon, the little shops on Central Avenue would close one by one. Gradually, games would end and the children would wander back home to find their mother donned in her apron, back at the stove preparing supper. Finally, the breadwinner would return home after a tiring day on the job.

The table was set, the food prepared, and the entire family would sit down for supper. The mother would talk about her day, the father would update her about his job, and the kids, if they had a good day, would talk about school. If there were no comments about school, it was time for a little parental probing to find out what went wrong in the classroom.

After the table was cleared, dishes washed and dried, homework done, and the children bedded down, the mother and father were back at the kitchen table. Here, they had their tea and what little time was left for themselves and private conversation. Soon afterwards, the doors were locked, the lights turned off, and a restful sleep would follow in preparation for the next day.

October 14, 1925 was no ordinary evening in a small, step-down apartment on Hancock Street. Emotions were running high. The adults were jittery, tense, and anxious. The three little boys could see the adults whispering and were confused by all the nervousness. They were doubly confused when their father ushered them upstairs to their grandmother's apartment and told them to be quiet.

Their mother, Marguerite Verity, had had a very difficult pregnancy and was now in labor. The doctor had been summoned earlier but still hadn't arrived. As a young city fireman, Frank Verity was trained to respond calmly to emergencies, but this was different. It was his wife that was in pain, his wife that was about to give birth to their fourth child. Frank was in and out the front door every few minutes, looking up and down Hancock Street for the doctor.

After what seemed like an interminable wait, a fancy black car turned off Central Avenue and came to a stop at 1149 Hancock Street. The doctor stepped out of the car dressed in a tuxedo. He made it very clear to Frank that he was running late for a formal dinner engagement. As he entered the apartment, the doctor announced that he hoped it would be a quick, uncomplicated delivery. The young fireman was not at all concerned about the doctor's dinner party. Frank just wanted him to take care of his wife.

It was not long before the doctor emerged from the bedroom and announced that Marguerite and Frank had their fourth son. The tension evaporated and everyone relaxed. The doctor left quickly and as his car pulled away from the curb, Frank vowed that this doctor would never have another Verity for a patient.

The three boys, who had heard so many stories about the stork, were called downstairs to meet their new little brother. They stood quietly at the bedside, smiled, and were not only amazed at how tiny their new brother was, but wondered how the stork had gotten into the apartment without them seeing it.

When Josie Reilly, a nurse and family friend, arrived to share the joy of the parents and their fourth soon, she quickly noticed a problem. "This baby is too pale. He's crying too much. Something is wrong." She quickly unwrapped the "bellyband" and realized that the doctor, in his haste, failed to tie the umbilical cord properly.

She told Frank to run up to the drug store on Central Avenue and get some "catgut." He sprinted up and back home as quickly as he could. Josie retied the cord, the bleeding stopped, and the crying soon stopped. The frightened parents hugged, the bystanders relaxed. The baby went to sleep. Josie Reilly had saved the day. The fourth Verity son had survived his first brush with danger.

As was her custom with each of her three older sons, Marguerite kept her newborn in a crib next to her bed so that she and Frank could watch over him. Her baby had a rough start in life and she was very concerned about him. Her concern proved warranted. About two weeks after his birth, while Frank was on duty at the firehouse, Marguerite was awakened, in the middle of the night, from a deep sleep by a strange noise.

She didn't know what had awakened her but she instinctively jumped out of bed, scooped the baby out of the crib, and ran into the hallway. In an instant, the entire bedroom ceiling came crashing down, covering her bed and filling the crib with huge, inch thick chunks of plaster. For the second time, her new son had barely escaped a most certain death.

Marguerite, a devout Catholic, credited her faith and her God to protecting her son. She had great devotion to Saint Gerard and always asked him to watch over all her babies. When Frank got home from work and saw the fallen ceiling, he agreed their fourth son should be named Gerard. A few days later, the baby and his godparents made their way up to Hancock Street to Saint Martin of Tours Church. It was official. The baby was baptized Gerard.

Following the baptism that Sunday afternoon, the little apartment at 1149 Hancock was overflowing with people. The parents, grandparents, godparents, aunts and uncles, friends and neighbors were all overjoyed. Marguerite was radiantly happy. Frank was passing out his favorite "White Owl" cigars. The three older Verity boys were busy raiding the cookies in the kitchen. And I, the center of attention, slept through it all!

Chapter Two

It soon became obvious that the little, ground floor apartment was too small and cramped for the growing Verity clan. Four boys all crowded into a single, tiny bedroom was neither healthy nor safe. As a fireman, Frank, on more than one occasion, experienced the terrible frustration of being unable to rescue children huddled together in a tiny, blazing apartment.

It was a long time and a lot of searching before my mother and father finally found a house that was both affordable and still located within the city limits. In 1928, the availability of affordable homes in the city was very limited. Word spread like wild fire that new homes were being built in Laurelton, a new development in southeast Queens. This was an answer to a prayer for Frank and Marguerite. They were thrilled when they saw the new homes under construction. Although my father did not make a high salary, as a city fireman he was considered to have job security. They got a mortgage for their two story, free standing stucco home. Because all the homes had similar red tiled roofs, they were commonly referred to as "Spanish" homes.

Frank and Marguerite couldn't wait for their home to be completed. What appealed to them was the privacy that came with a backyard, a driveway, and a side door. For the mother and housewife, it was a great place to raise children. For my father, the Long Island Railroad stopped at the nearby Rosedale station which meant an easy commute to his job. My older brothers saw the unlimited possibilities in the open spaces. It was 1928 when the Verity family moved into their new home on 232 Street.

Less than a year later, on Black Tuesday, October 1929, the Stock Market crashed. The Great Depression was taking its toll in Laurelton. New home owners had to abandon their dream. "For Sale" signs were springing up on every street. Although civil service workers had job security, to meet expenses my father had to moonlight as a plumber. Of course, he wasn't the only civil servant in Laurelton to experience financial stress in trying to make "ends meet." He had plenty of company. There were so many uniformed cops and firemen commuting from the Rosedale Station that they were referred to as the Blue Army.

Time continued to march on and I eventually found myself a "big brother." I was five when my brother Harold was born in March 1931. From that time on, we became known in the neighborhood as the five Verity boys, or the fireman's sons: Bill, Jack, Bud, Gerard, and Harold. We had a normal childhood; a mixture of good days and bad days, fun times and sad times. We had our share of mumps and measles, chicken pox, poison ivy, broken limbs and blackened eyes – but nothing life threatening. It seemed that no matter what happened to us, once the excitement was over Mom would say, "Thank God, it could have been worse."

One by one, as each of us grew old enough, we became paper-boys and delivered the Long Island Press. Whatever we earned from the Press, we turned into the house. Whatever we earned as tips, Mom allowed us to keep. This was a smart move on Mom's part – we not only had an incentive to please the customers but more importantly, in our eyes, tips paid our way into the "Itch" on Saturday where we could see a double feature, a serial, and cartoons. All this for a dime with change left over for a trip to Robbin's Candy Store on Merrick Road. We learned the value of money at an early age.

Along with being paper-boys, we also all became altar boys. We served in our local parish, Saint Clare's in Rosedale, which was about a quarter of a mile from our house. Being an altar boy meant attending Saturday morning meetings in order to memorize Latin prayers and practice the proper way to serve Mass. Our instructors, who took themselves very seriously, were usually high school students who acted more like drill sergeants in the armed forces. When the training was complete and our Latin tests passed, Mom and Pop imposed their iron clad rule – "Never be late for or miss a Mass assignment and make sure your hands are washed and hair combed." I'm not certain about the clean hands or combed hair, but I am sure that I never missed an assignment. I was like a little mail carrier - neither rain, nor sleet, nor snow would deter me from my appointed Mass.

Attending public school as an altar boy had its advantages. On Holy Days, we got out of class to serve Mass. We also loved funerals. They too, got us excused from class and, even better, most funeral directors tipped each server a quarter. Then, there were the weddings – the best possible assignments. Unfortunately, for the most part, there seemed to be an unwritten law that only high school servers got the Saturday weddings, where the Best Man impressed the wedding party by reaching a little more deeply into his pockets to tip the servers.

In recognition of our faithful service, all altar boys were treated, once a year, to an all day outing at Steeple Chase Park in Coney Island. At Christmas time, the Pastor, who never learned our names, also presented each of us with a new hair brush, comb, and finger nail file. Not such a subtle hint, but still a welcomed gift!

The only time I came close to being expelled from the "Altar Boys," was at a weekday Mass. The pastor had just been elevated to the rank of Monsignor. He wasted no time getting outfitted in his new red cassock and fancy biretta with red "pom-pom" on top. At the start of Mass, the biretta is taken off and placed on the first of three steps leading up to the altar. In the course of the Mass, the server changes the large prayer book from one side of the altar to the other. My co-server, Billy Ryan, very reverently and correctly carried the book down the three steps, genuflected on the floor, and took the missal up the steps to the far side of the altar. On the way up, however, Billy evidently stepped on and flattened the Monsignor's new biretta. Unbeknownst to the Monsignor who was facing the altar, I quickly tried to restore his pride and joy to its original shape.

I don't know if it was a case of nerves, but Billy and I started to snicker and the more we tried to stifle our laughs, the worse it got. The Monsignor was enraged and distracted by our futile attempts to muffle our nervous laughter. Fake coughs, bitten lips, etc., could not fool him.

On our return to the sacristy, the Monsignor failed to notice his damaged hat and refrained from asking what caused our outburst. He was always cranky to begin with, but this day he was furious. He asked for an apology and told us we would never serve again if we couldn't control ourselves. He emphasized that this was his final warning.

On the way home, Billy and I reenacted the mishap and laughed till tears rolled down our cheeks. It was only years later that I told my parents about it.

Chapter Three

Certain days from my childhood stand out in my memory
- sometimes because there was great joy; sometimes because
of great sadness; and sometimes because a great lesson was
learned. I can remember, when I was about ten, I was home
alone with my mother. In those days, there were no supermarkets
or malls. The little stores that lined Merrick Road served our
basic needs – the deli, butcher shops, bakery, drugstore, candy
store, and hardware.

A few times each week, peddlers would ring the side door
bell, open their valise and display their wares for the housewives.
Very often, they would come at the most inappropriate times.
On this particular day, my mother was busy at the washboard
in the cellar.

When the bell rang, I went to the side door and opened it.
A poorly dressed man was there empty handed, no valise. He
just looked at me and softly, almost apologetically, said, "I'm
hungry. Could I have something to eat?"

Trying to save my mother a trip upstairs and not sure how to reply, I simply said, "My mother's not home." I really wasn't a good liar and I think the man knew it. He didn't say a word and slowly walked away. My mother stopped doing the laundry and called upstairs to me, "Who was at the door?" I answered, "Some man who said he was hungry and asked for something to eat. I told him you weren't home."

For a ten year old, I thought I had handled the situation very well. My mother strongly disagreed! She came flying up the cellar steps and angrily told me to run after the hungry man and bring him back! I was so embarrassed. I still remember her words, "We don't have much, but thank God we have enough."

He wasn't asking for money, just food. I caught up to him and brought him back home. Mom gave him bacon and eggs and a big cup of coffee. He gobbled it down, thanked Mom profusely, gave me a little smile and we never saw him again.

Mom reminded me simply that Jesus said, "Whatever you do for the poor or the hungry, you do for me." I learned an important lesson that would stick with me for a lifetime.

As far as I can remember, none of the Veritys, not Mom, Pop, or my brothers – were ever "holy rollers." As a matter of fact, if any pranks were pulled off in the immediate neighborhood, usually at least one of the Verity boys was blamed. The odds were not in our favor. But still, religion was an important part of our lives. For us, the Sunday morning routine never changed. We delivered our papers by eight, came home, and cleaned up. Sunday Mass was an absolute must, no exception. If we were ever sick enough to skip Mass, which was rare, then there could be no miraculous recovery. There would be no going out to play later or staying up to listen to the radio after supper. To fake sickness on Sunday morning was to be subjected to "house arrest" and the possibility of consuming one of Mom's universal remedies – sulfur and molasses or a gigantic dose of mineral oil.

Since Saint Clare's had no parish school, us public school kids were expected to attend the nine o'clock children's Mass, unless we were scheduled to serve a later Mass. When Mass ended, there was no escaping Sunday school. Our Sunday school teacher corralled us together, stopped traffic on Brookville Boulevard, and marched us into the parish hall across the street. Sunday morning was definitely God's time!

When Pop wasn't on duty at the firehouse, he and Mom would go to the eight o'clock Mass together. On the rare weekends when Pop had both days off, he would assemble his sons late Saturday afternoon and march us over to confession. He wasn't big on preaching religion, but he certainly led by example. If he caught us doing something wrong, his favorite expression was, "Don't forget to mention it in confession."

While Pop was active in the Holy Name Society of the Fire Department, neither he nor my Mom were active in the local parish societies. Mom doled out a nickel to each of us on Sunday morning for the collection basket. Like a broken record, each Sunday morning the pastor would pass the collection baskets and state, "Give as your means will permit." My parents gave faithfully and generously to a fund for a parish school which never materialized until all of their sons were adults.

Occasionally, after Sunday dinner, we would walk up to Merrick Road and catch a "Bee Line Bus" into Jamaica to visit my father's parents. I can still see my grandfather's "handle bar" mustache which would tickle us when he greeted us with a kiss. He was a hardy old bird who was a carpenter and boat builder, originally from Amityville, Long Island. He was Protestant, never converted to Catholicism, but never interfered with or objected to his five children being raised Catholic. My grandmother Nee Mary Goggin, was born in Ireland. I remember her as a delicate little woman who, during our visits, would sit alongside my mother and continuously smile or chuckle at the crazy antics of her five grandsons. Grandma was a great lady and had all of our respect.

My maternal grandparents followed my mother from Bushwick and bought a house next door in Laurelton. Ma Jule, as we called her, was a great cook. She was forever cooking nut bread and rice pudding for us. My mother's father, Richard, was a jolly, little "roly-poly" man who was employed as a silver smith. If he had ever grown a white beard, he would have been a perfect Santa Claus.

I remember Grandpa Richard especially for the little fishing trips he took us on. He taught us the fine art of drop fishing along the shores of salt water creeks. No fancy rods and reels, just string, a hook and sinker, and a little bait. What really excited us were his demonstrations of how to lure crabs into a long handle net with nothing more than a piece of bait tied to a string. When I think back, it's a wonder none of us died from some horrible disease from eating the crab out of those muddy creeks.

My maternal grandfather was the first of my grandparents to die. He died suddenly. I loved him dearly and was crushed by his death. He was waked at home and when I saw him in the coffin, the only explanation that made any sense to me was that God called him to heaven because he was such a good man. All I really understood was that I loved him and would miss him terribly.

Chapter Four

A few years later, following in the foot steps of my older brothers, I was able to convince my parents to allow me to go on my favorite hike to Rusty's Creek with my friends. After packing a few peanut butter and jelly sandwiches, drop line, and bait, we set out for the south Rosedale swamps. Obviously, the brackish water was named "Rusty's" due to its unique shade of brown. But after a two mile hike in the hot sun, we still couldn't wait to peel off our clothes and dive in the creek, not knowing what awaited us beneath the surface. At low tide, the smell from the muddy bottom was horrendous but we considered this a small price to pay for our secret, private beach. The biggest challenge of the hike was the attempt to conceal our sunburn and our dirty, matted hair on the return home. Not long into the summer, Rusty's ended up on Mom's "out of bounds" list. My brothers and I often asked, "How did Mom find out?" Now, in retrospect, I realize that Mom didn't have a sixth sense. She didn't need one. We probably reeked of dead fish!

There was never a day when we had nothing to do. If it wasn't fishing, crabbing, or skinny dipping, it was choosing sides for baseball or football. The block was our universe. The road was a ribbon of two lanes of concrete with shoulders that were a mixture of dust, ashes, and gravel; all hemmed in by cement curbs. The block served us well. In the summer, it was our baseball field, in the fall, our football stadium, and in the winter, our battle field for snowball fights. The neighborhood girls were of no interest to us at this point. They kept to themselves and I soon learned that many of them considered themselves "spies." Their brothers warned me that nothing gave them greater pleasure than to report any improper speech or conduct to their parents. I didn't know about this; I had no sisters.

In between innings of baseball or during football time-outs, the curb was our dugout, our sidelines, and the occasional conference room for all kinds of stories and jokes. It was also the highly secret planning center for Halloween pranks. One late summer day, Mr. Schneider, nicknamed "Crabby," confiscated our one and only baseball which brought our game to a screeching halt. He was up on a ladder painting his house. One of our fly balls almost hit him as it bounced off his house. He didn't have any kids of his own and we often wondered if he had ever been a kid himself. He was the meanest old man on the block. He got down from the ladder, picked up the ball, turned toward us like the Statue of Liberty, and held it high for all of us to see. Then, like the cat that ate the canary, he gave us a prissy, little smirk, dramatically put the ball in his pocket, and disappeared into his house. That was the end of our baseball season.

We were furious but we wouldn't dare show disrespect to an adult. We might have muttered more colorful language, but that was it. However, we did immediately hold a highly sensitive curbside strategy session. Halloween wasn't that far away and we now had our prime target. We almost forgot about the confiscated ball, once we began planning our retaliation for Crabby. I'm sure my part in the retaliation found its way into my weekly confession. Nevertheless, it was worth it when Crabby opened his door on Halloween to find a paper bag on fire. We anxiously watched as he stomped on it and then, laughed hysterically as he realized it was filled with dog droppings. It was one of our proudest moments.

We were an ecumenical group – a fairly even mixture of Protestants, Catholics and Jews. We were sometimes little curbside moral theologians. Early one Saturday morning, we were stretched along the curb waiting for our friend, Bruce, to bring the one decent football on the block. As we sat there, the milkman was going from house to house making his weekly collection. He stopped his horse and wagon right across from us. His horse began to urinate and we all became hysterical, laughing and rolling on the ground. Comments started flying, "What a leak," "What a piss."

When the horse moved on and we settled down, the word "piss" came up for discussion. It wasn't an everyday word in our vocabulary and one of the Catholic kids wondered if he should mention it in his confession. Protestants, Jews, and Catholics agreed they wouldn't say "piss" in front of their mothers. My cousin, who was visiting from Brooklyn, ended our discussion because his Brooklyn friends not only said "piss" but a lot worse than that. My cousin spoke authoritatively when it came to cursing and swearing. Compared to us, he was in the major league of slang.

When the question of confession came up, my Jewish and Protestant friends just listened and asked questions. They had no worries about confessing sins. They got off easy. I didn't know if that was good or bad. The priest who heard my confession every Saturday was very kind and patient. He never yelled or scolded. In fact, when I told him what names I called my brothers during fights, I sometimes thought I heard a little chuckle. He was my idea of a great priest. Going into the confessional was always a little embarrassing but I always felt good and clean coming out. It was something like our Saturday night bath. While I always thought Pop's scrubbing routine was pretty rough, the end result made me feel refreshed and clean.

One late fall afternoon, when football ended, our little gang sat on the curb waiting to be called for supper. We got into one of our typical bragging sessions over who had the best father. Each of us had good reasons for thinking our father was the best – a lot of thought and heart went into these debates. Suddenly, my father rounded the corner and came walking down the street on his way home from work. His timing couldn't have been better. There he was in his blue dress uniform – his silver buttoned overcoat, and his fire cap which made him look ten feet tall. As far as I was concerned, that image was proof positive – my father was the best! I jumped up, ran to him, and proudly accompanied him into the house.

Pop was a big, strong man and no stranger to hard work. In addition to being a fireman, he moonlighted as the neighborhood plumber. He was always in demand. He fixed faucets, installed new pipes, cleaned clogged traps – whatever it took to help pay the bills. Never having owned a car, he carried a big, very heavy canvas toolbag which would have been a challenge for any of his boys to lift. I was in awe of his strength.

Basically, my father, Frank, was a quiet, gentle giant who buried his emotions. But despite his quiet nature, he was always quick to respond to any tenderness extended to him with a warm smile, chuckle or a hug. Unfortunately, because he was unassuming and more inclined to fade into the background, he was often taken for granted.

Occasionally, Pop would get side tracked on the way home from work and stop off at Killarney's Bar. If Pop had a "few too many" and was late for supper, he would get quite a tongue lashing from tiny Marge. Whenever I heard Mom and Pop raise their voices, it tore me apart. I loved them both deeply and was unable to take sides. Whenever there were harsh words or flare ups, I would get nervous and couldn't wait for peace to be restored.

Mom, or Marge as she was called, was a tiny woman whose family and house always came first. She was outspoken in defense of her family, emotional, and filled with boundless energy. If she wasn't in the basement scrubbing clothes at the tub, she was at the kitchen stove. If she wasn't cleaning house, she was carrying groceries home from Merrick Road. She had few outside interests, whether it be the school, the community, or parish societies. Her life was her family and her house. She made the house rules and Pop was the enforcer.

Mom was an excellent cook. She would pile the plates high. She used to say, "I love to see all my men eat." When the food platter was passed around she would say "Take what you want, but eat what you take" or "Don't let your eyes be bigger than your stomach – you can always come back for more." Mom always hated to see us waste food and constantly reminded us of the poor who had little to eat.

Mom might have ruled the stove but Pop ruled the sink. He had a regular ritual after supper. When he got up from the table, he would don a large white apron that we were sure he was awarded by the bartender of Killarney's Pub. He would fill the sink with sudsy water, do the dishes, pots and pans and either whistle to himself or sing, "I love the flowers and the sunshine." All was well in the Verity household when Pop sang at the sink.

One time Pop broke a dish at the sink and Mom gave him a real tongue lashing for it. He didn't say a word but silently took off his apron, hung it up, and walked away from his sudsy water, not to return for what seemed like an eternity. It was his own, personal "work stoppage." Needless to say, little Marge never criticized his dish washing technique again. A few weeks later, when he once again reached for the apron and began to whistle and sing, we knew the strike was over.

I can remember two occasions when supper was a disaster. Mom had just piled everyone's plate high with her creamy mashed potatoes. When she returned to the stove, I snuck a big spoonful of horse radish into my little brother's "mashies." Bill, Jack, Bud, and I waited for Harold's reaction as he took a big mouthful of potatoes. His reaction was instantaneous. He screamed, and spit a mouthful of sabotaged food all over the table. We all howled with laughter until Mom screamed and chased me with the nearest weapon at hand – her large wooden spoon. The chase was followed by her most effective threat, "Wait until your father gets home!"

My brother Jack was the family comedian. Jack was always good for a laugh. Because he had the biggest paper route, he received the most tips and consequently, always had more spending money than the rest of us. One day he bought a "whoopee" cushion. We never tired of it. Jack kept us rolling on the floor each time he deflated it. We couldn't wait for supper. Jack made sure to sit next to Pop. As Pop sat down, Jack slid the cushion from under the table onto my father's chair. An unsuspecting Pop lowered himself onto the whoopee cushion and it released the largest fart sound we had ever heard. Mom was startled; Pop froze and turned beet red. We all laughed but Pop got furious, grabbed the cushion, and threw it into the furnace. Jack plead guilty and was sent to bed without supper.

The rest of us ate in a silence that was peppered with snickers every time we made eye contact with each other. We felt bad for Jack and managed to sneak food to him, which I'm sure Mom and Pop pretended not to see. After all, we were only following their instructions, "Brothers should always stick together."

The house became quiet after the dishes were washed and dried, and the pots and pans put away. It was also a time for homework. It was a time for Mom and Pop to relax. Pop would light up a White Owl cigar and tell Mom about the job. It was the most talking Pop would do all day.

For a good part of his career, Pop worked in Rescue # 4 in Woodside. It was not unusual for him to come home with cuts and burns. A few times he had to be admitted to the hospital. But with all his daily stress, only one time did I see him choke up with tears. He told Mom how he had rushed into a burning apartment to rescue a little girl. He said he was too late and the little girl died in his arms. Until that moment, I had always seen Pop as a big, rugged fireman. Now, I saw him as a gentle, brave hero who wept for the little girl he was unable to save.

Chapter Five

1938 was a year of rapid change in the Verity household. My oldest brother, Bill, was commuting into Manhattan where he worked in an office. Jack graduated from High School and succeeded in finding a job in Robbin's Dry Dock, a shipyard in Red Hook, Brooklyn. Jack bought a "Model A" Ford for less than a hundred dollars. Bill switched jobs and together, he and Jack, would leave for the Brooklyn waterfront at six o'clock every morning. Of course, Mom was up before them making them breakfast and a packed lunch. She'd then stand at the front window and watch Jack's little car, with its rumble seat, as it drove off out of sight.

Bud was still attending Andrew Jackson High School and was able to find a part time job as an usher in the Merrick Theatre in Jamaica. The three older Verity boys were beyond delivering papers and serving on the altar. Their lives were changing rapidly; they were serving a whole new world.

Because I inherited Bud's paper route, he gave me his red Hawthorne bike, which he bought from Montgomery Ward. He took good care of it. It was bright red, had what were called balloon tires, and a basket large enough to hold the route's papers. Bud trained me and introduced me to his customers. Taking over his route was a challenge. He was a good business man. He set high standards. His customers respected him and tipped him well. I had big shoes to fill and I took the job seriously. I became proficient in delivery, being able to pedal the big Hawthorne non-stop while improving my accuracy in tossing the paper up to the top step of a customer's stoop.

The local A&P on Merrick Road was no supermarket by any stretch of the imagination, but it was the biggest store around. It was a real "bee hive" of activity on Saturday morning. Housewives would enter the store empty handed and exit loaded down with bundles. Few families owned cars, so husbands and children would tag along and share the burden. I would accompany my mother and wait outside with my trusty Hawthorne. When she exited, I would fill my basket and pedal shopping bags home.

While waiting outside, I noticed many women overburdened with packages on their return home. I recognized a lot of these women as neighbors and customers on my paper route. I got a brilliant idea and went in to see Fred Mooney, the store manager. He knew my parents and me from our many trips to his store. He was a real gentleman. I asked him if he would allow me to attach a sign to my basket announcing a ten cent charge for "home delivery" of groceries. He gave me the green light. I was in a new business venture. Each week, business grew and I would shuttle back and forth between the store and the customers' homes. Everyone was happy. The women didn't have to carry the packages, their husbands were happy to stay home, and I had what I considered a fantastic income.

Unfortunately, my delivery business was short lived. So many competitors arrived on the scene with their bikes that customers started to complain about a "tripping hazard" on the sidewalk. People could barely get around all of the parked bikes. Reluctantly, Mr. Mooney told me that bikers could no longer congregate in front of the store. I could tell he felt genuinely bad about ending my new business. It came as no surprise to me when he eventually resigned from his management position to enter the seminary and become a priest. He was the first person I knew personally that chose to enter a seminary. I remember feeling encouraged as I realized that ordinary people could become priests.

By this time, I was going on thirteen. My body was maturing; my thoughts and interests were changing. And ever since I had inherited my Hawthorne bike, my little world was expanding. Gradually, my friends and I yielded the curb to my seven year old brother, Harold, and his friends. I guess his four older brothers had earned the trust of our parents, because Harold was given a lot more liberty than the rest of us. He was more adventurous, took longer hikes, and was far more precocious. Because of the six year gap between him and me, Harold always got new clothes and new toys – no "hand me downs." He reaped all the benefits of being the youngest and the last to arrive.

Both Harold and I attended Public School #156. At this point in time, he was in the first grade and I was in the seventh. Harold enjoyed life. He had a good time wherever he was - even in school – so much so that his teacher began sending notes home. This upset my mother and father. They'd never had a "discipline" problem before.

As September approached, Mom got more and more concerned about Harold's school work. She referred to him as the "young rip." More than once, Mom expressed her desire for Harold to attend a "Sister" school where there would be strict discipline. Harold wasn't dumb, but having a good time came first and his lessons second.

I found myself trying to "fix" the worrisome situation and I soon had a plan. As an altar boy, I thought I might have a little pull with a local priest. I told Mom I was going to take a bike ride up to Saint Boniface Parish in Elmont, about three miles away. I rang the rectory bell and asked the housekeeper if I could speak to the Pastor. In a few minutes, Father Rath came into the parlor. I guess he could see that I was scared and he put me at ease right away. I told Father Rath that I was an altar boy in Saint Clare's and asked if my little brother and I could enroll in Saint Boniface School. He laughed and said Father Goeller, the pastor of Saint Clare's, "would have been wiser to build a school for the children rather than a Cathedral for the adults."

We walked outside and I showed him my prize possession, the Hawthorne. I explained that I could ride both myself and Harold, everyday, if he would let us enroll in the school. Without hesitation, Father Rath directed me to the convent and told me to inform Sister Ignatia that Harold and I would be attending Saint Boniface. I was very proud of my accomplishment and raced home to share the good news with Mom and Pop.

The transfer and transition from P.S. 156 to Saint Boniface was a very smooth one, despite how different Saint Boniface was. We were going from a large three story city school to a little country school. We left behind a large, crowded classroom and entered a class of twelve. The whole atmosphere was different. The pastor was very kind, the Sisters most caring and welcoming. From the start, it felt like the right move.

Looking back, it was Harold's misbehavior that prompted the whole change. Ironically, the "young rip" was a hit with the Sisters. Harold had a very angelic look about him and the Sisters took an instant liking to him. Mom and Pop couldn't believe it three months later when the Sisters selected angel faced, Harold, to be the Baby Jesus in the school Christmas pageant! From "Peck's Bad Boy" to the Baby Jesus – it sounded like something out of the movie, "The Bells of St. Mary," but it really did happen. By the time that first year at Saint Boniface came to a close, we knew we had made the right decision and looked forward to a long summer.

The summer of '38 was a memorable one. As its conclusion rapidly approached, my friends and I were determined to squeeze as much fun as we could into the final few weeks. Four of us, who had bikes, became like a junior version of the "Hells Angels." We were a little bicycle club constantly exploring the neighboring towns. One of our favorite destinations was Mitchell Field where we would park our bikes outside the fence and watch the military planes come and go. It was so exciting.

On clear, warm days, Valley Stream State Park was our top priority. Valley Stream was about three miles away in Nassau County. It was a lake, with two large rafts available to swimmers. Each raft was about thirty feet long – one for diving, the other for sliding. Lifeguards controlled all water activities and the State Troopers controlled the shore activities. Admission to the Park was free before 9 a.m. Promptly at nine, the open gates were locked. The troopers would position themselves at the turn-stiles and a ten cent admission charge was suddenly enforced.

The "Four Musketeers," as we called ourselves, would meet promptly at 8 a.m. at the Twin Ponds Bakery. For a nickel, we had a choice of two buns or one spice cake with raisins and chocolate icing. The spice cake, my favorite, was like a large muffin, very filling and enough to get me through lunch. We operated on a very tight, strict schedule. As soon as our purchases were complete, we would jump on our trusty bikes and pedal like mad down Merrick Road. Upon arrival, we'd park, chain our bikes, and run like crazy through the open gates. We staked out our favorite spot on the beach with our clothes, lunch bags and smelly sneakers. And as we made a mad dash for the water in our woolen trunks, someone would always yell, "Last one in is a rotten egg!"

We would spend ninety percent of the next five hours in the water and only ten percent clowning around on the beach. We would have had to be blind not to notice that the girls our age were developing into young ladies. This accounted for a certain amount of clowning around on the beach and for a definite change in topics of conversation.

After our final plunge into the water at two o'clock, we would pick up our clothes and with our trunks still dripping, we would run to our bikes. We then would peddle to the woods across Merrick Road and quickly strip off our swim trunks, put on our pants, and be off to the Press office to pick up our papers for delivery. We started the summer with a pink sunburn and ended it with a golden tan. It was a happy, healthy routine.

Late in August, my mother planned to make meat loaf for supper and asked me to pick up the meat at the butcher's before delivering my papers. This meant cutting my beach time by a half hour and making the trip home alone. I followed our regular routine and went to our regular spot in the woods to get out of my wet trunks.

I was no sooner out of my wet trunks and pulling up my pants when I was completely startled by a man who appeared from nowhere. He must have been hiding in the bushes. He smiled, spoke softly, and placed three or four black and white pictures in my hand. They were the dirtiest, most graphic pictures of men and women having sex. I was dumbstruck and frightened. When I looked away from the pictures, the crazed man was exposed and fully aroused.

Even though all of this took place within a minute and no physical contact was made, I felt like a scared rabbit trapped by a ferocious animal. I threw the filthy pictures on the ground at his feet and ran to my bike. The man angrily shouted, "Where are you going?" I shouted back, "Home!" He asked "Where's home?" Terrified, I couldn't get out of there fast enough and in a panic, rode west with my heart pounding.

As I rode frantically along Merrick Road, I almost expected to see the man behind the wheel of every car overtaking me. Fortunately, I made it to the butcher's shop and home, without seeing him again. When I finally arrived home, there were police cars on my block and many neighbors were standing around. This horrible day quickly grew even worse, when my mother told me that a neighbor had committed suicide and was hanging in his cellar. I felt awful but was still shaken from my encounter in the woods. With all the activity on the street, my mother never noticed how upset and frightened I still was from this unforgettable encounter with a pedophile.

I knew I did nothing wrong. I didn't feel guilty but I decided that this whole episode would have to be kept secret. I was too embarrassed to talk to my parents about it. How would I find words to describe it when we never spoke about sex at home? My only sex education came from very limited curbside discussions with my friends.

Furthermore, had I mentioned this horrible experience to my parents, I knew Valley Stream would be declared off limits forever. So, I kept quiet and continued to go to Valley Stream, but I never entered the woods alone again. And thankfully, I never saw that awful man again. None of my friends ever mentioned having a similar experience. I was glad the summer was over and did my best to forget that man, but he remained a frightening memory for a long time.

After school started I met Father Rath in the school yard one day. He asked me how I was doing and I told him that religion was my worst subject. I told him that my classmates, having spent seven years in Catholic school, all had the Baltimore Catechism memorized. Having a religion class in school was a new experience for me. He could see that I was discouraged and jokingly told me that I had an advantage over all my classmates because my last name was "Verity." He asked me if I knew what Verity meant. I didn't.

Father Rath explained that Verity means truth and that I should be very proud of it. And I instantly was proud. Father Rath was a great priest and always managed to make me smile. During my short time in Saint Boniface, he not only knew my name but also offered me the honor of serving at his Mass. Father Rath accomplished more and had a greater impact on me during that brief period, than my pastor in Saint Clare's had during my three years as an altar boy.

In the fall of that same year, our house was full of relatives celebrating Thanksgiving. I had just turned thirteen and as we were all gathered around the table, one of my uncles asked each of the kids what they wanted to be when they grew up. I don't remember how my brothers and cousins answered the question, but when my turn came, I answered, "I want to be either a pilot or a priest." All the adults laughed when my uncle commented, "Either way, you're aiming high."

My desire to be a pilot was easily explained. I was fascinated by the army planes that I would watch with my friends at Mitchell Field. But, this was the first time that I had verbally expressed an interest in being a priest. I could not explain this hidden attraction to the priesthood. I'm sure my admiration for Father Rath had a lot to do with it.

Chapter Six

During the late 1930s, we had "split-sessions" in school. This meant each grade would begin in January and conclude in December. The December after my fourteenth birthday, in October of 1939, I graduated from grade school. The Sisters and Father Rath all encouraged each of their graduates to enter Catholic high school. I chose Saint Francis Prep in Brooklyn. Saint Francis was a relatively easy commute. First, I'd take the Long Island Railroad from Rosedale to Flatbush Avenue and then I'd have only a half hour walk. The commute was no problem, but the monthly tuition of ten dollars, plus train fare, represented a big expense in 1940. But Mom and Pop made it happen. They always managed to scrape together the money their kids needed.

My first day at Saint Francis was a memorable one. On entering the school, I asked a few older guys, probably seniors, where I needed to go to register. They pointed to the last doorway on the right. When I opened the door it was the janitor's closet.

I could hear them laughing at the gullible freshman. I knew I was in another league, now.

The Brooklyn kids were streetwise but the Franciscan Brothers were always a step ahead. Brother Charles was a no nonsense principal, a great disciplinarian. Brother James, our algebra teacher, was my favorite. Even with his quiet, soft-spoken manner, he never had a discipline problem in his classroom. The Franciscan Brothers were dedicated teachers who always treated us fairly. If they gave us a smack in the back of the head, there were no arguments or excuses – we accepted that we deserved what we got. We did have a lay teacher, nicknamed "Happy Hands" because he was too quick with the "ruler." Although "Happy Hands" never struck me, I still resented him smacking the others. He seemed to enjoy it. When the Brothers hit, it was well deserved. I couldn't always say the same for "Happy Hands."

Saint Francis Prep was no architectural gem. It was a tired, old fashioned, worn out building that only the Franciscans, with their dedicated pledge of poverty, could bear. The subterranean gym had such a low ceiling that it was impossible to shoot a basketball. The famous St. Francis "Terriers" had to practice in the nearby college gym. The toilets were located in a separate building in the school yard and there was a stampede to them after every lunch period. But no one ever complained. The Prep had a fantastic school spirit and I know I could have finished four years there with ease.

But by the time I had arrived at Saint Francis, the thought of becoming a missionary priest had been nagging at me for six months. The first person I sought out was Brother James. He was a good listener and suggested that I talk about my interest with Father Rath, immediately. It was June of 1940 and if I was to transfer from Saint Francis to a seminary in September, there was no time to spare.

I told Father Rath that I wanted to be a foreign missionary priest. He told me a Passionist Missionary was going to visit Saint Boniface in a week and suggested I talk with him. I knew nothing about Passionists but when the visiting missionary told me that the Passionists were staffing a mission to Hunan, China, that was all I needed to know.

Father Emmanuel, the Passionist, informed me that the life of a missionary is quite difficult. He also told me that recently, some Passionist priests were killed by Chinese bandits. But none of his stories discouraged me. The more I heard about foreign missions, the more I wanted it. He contacted the Passionist minor seminary in Dunkirk, New York and had the necessary information forwarded to me.

After my chat with Father Emmanuel, I rushed home to tell Mom and Pop of my desire to enter the seminary in September. I wasn't sure what kind of reaction my parents would have, but they didn't seem surprised. When I assured them that I had been thinking about it for a long time and was sure that I wanted it, they both gave their consent. They both said they would be honored if one of their sons became a priest but stressed that it had to be my decision. Mom kept saying and Pop nodded in agreement, "This is your home. If you're ever not happy in the seminary, we want you to come home."

At supper that night, I broke the news to my brothers. They asked many questions and I was unable to answer most of them. Overall, they seemed bewildered by the whole thing. I would be the first of the five Verity boys to leave home. After the shock wore off, they started with the jokes. "Father Gerard, would you hear my confession?" We had a lot of good laughs. The initial shock was over but the reality of my leaving home became more obvious as September grew closer.

The rest of the summer flew by. All the paper work, the application, school transcripts, completed medical exams, etc., had to be finished. We had to go to Montgomery Ward in Jamaica to buy a footlocker and we had a shopping list of items that would eventually fill it. A week before leaving, Railway Express picked up the footlocker and shipped it to Dunkirk. Dunkirk was on the shores of Lake Erie, over four hundred miles from my home and my family.

Departure day was the Tuesday after Labor Day. My brothers were quiet and solemn. Each of them wished me well, gave me a few slaps on the back, and walked me to the sidewalk. My parents then walked me to Merrick Road where we caught a bus into Jamaica. This was followed by a quiet "El" ride into Grand Central. I felt a mixture of excitement and sadness. Once at Grand Central, there were a few minutes of small talk and last minute instructions. Then, I received a kiss from Mom, a hug from Pop, and I answered the final call to board the Empire State Express. I took one last look back and, as I did, I saw Pop put his arms around Mom.

Once on board, I met Joe Byrne from Queens Village. Even though he was five years older and entering his second year of college, we had a lot in common. We came from similar size families, both of our fathers were civil service workers – mine a fireman, his a cop – and we both wanted to be priests. I liked Joe, immediately. He helped me devour the sandwiches and homemade cake supplied by my mother. Eight hours and four hundred miles later, we got off the train in quiet, little Dunkirk – a place totally different from our hometown of New York.

Chapter Seven

When we arrived at Holy Cross Seminary, called the "Prep," we were greeted by about twelve Passionist priests and brothers and about twenty young seminarians, or postulants, who looked like mini missionaries. It was a very warm welcome – lots of happy, smiling faces. But all of these people in black, were somewhat disarming. I had never met so many total strangers who were so friendly, so soon. I had some doubts about fitting into this group of happy, holy teens. Their greeting was overwhelming.

Following the greeting, we were separated into groups according to age and grades, and each group was given a guided tour. At this point, I met my new classmates. All together, there were twelve of us. I was the only "New Yorker." The others came from Boston and Worcester, Pittsburgh and Scranton, and there were even a couple from across Lake Erie – Canada. It was a mixed group with all different accents, each looking to make a friend.

Our first stop on the tour was the Junior Dorm with enough beds and linens to accommodate the freshmen, sophomores, and juniors. The Senior Dorm, which was "out of bounds" for us, was restricted to high school seniors, college freshman, and college sophomores. We were given our assigned lockers, where we placed our luggage. I immediately noticed that the lockers had no locks! For the New Yorker, this came as quite a shock.

The dorm was on the third floor, over looking the seventy acres of seminary property. The property bordered on Lake Erie, which looked more like an ocean to me than a lake. Down below, we could see a baseball diamond, a football field, and handball courts. The sight of the ball fields helped me to relax and to realize that seminarians were normal guys and that just maybe I would fit in. Our next eye opener, was the men's room next to the dorm. It was old fashioned – about fifteen urinals along one wall and about ten private toilets. This was the first time I ever saw this type of wooden water container with its long chain dangling, just within reach of the occupant. With a pull of the chain, the flush came with a roar. We all laughed when this antiquated room was called the "Jakes." The neighboring washroom was lined with sinks and mirrors on one side and towels (each with a name above it) hanging along the other wall. It was very plain but functional. Shower rooms were located on the first floor, close to the gym and ball fields.

Next, we were shown the large dining hall, filled with long rectangular tables lined up in three separate rows. We were informed that this room was called the "refectory" – a new word to be remembered. We were told that meals were eaten in silence except on special feast days. During the silence, a spiritual book on the life of a saint was read by the college seminarians. This was a bit of a shocker for us. We were led to the table assigned to us. Our young guide, who at that moment wanted to inject a little holiness into the tour, said we twelve would be like the twelve apostles seated at the "Last Supper." He said we, too, would probably change the world.

My classmate, Porky Joyce, and I weren't prepared for this kind of "holy talk." We glanced at each other, smiled, and rolled our eyes. Once again, I had been wondering if I would fit in, but Porky's reaction was reassuring. We became fast friends from that moment on.

Next stop, was the chapel. It was very impressive but unlike any church I'd ever seen before. Instead of regular pews facing the altar, there were two rows of pews or "lecterns" (another new word) around the sides and rear of the chapel. We were told all prayers would be in Latin, and that we would chant a portion of the "Divine Office" everyday. Now, I was really concerned. I thought my years as an altar boy would have prepared me better for all of this. I had the unsettling feeling that I was entering into a whole new world that I was completely unprepared for. But as I looked at the expressions on the faces of my classmates, I knew I wasn't alone.

Our next stop on the tour was the study hall. It had about a hundred simple, wooden desks lined up in five rows, which stretched from the front of the hall to the back. As freshmen, we were assigned to the desks up front. The oldest students had the desks in the back. Silence was to be observed at all time in the study hall.

After each of us got seated at our assigned desks, Father Basil Cavanaugh introduced himself as our Prefect. Father Gregory Flynn was our Vice Prefect. It was a happy meeting for the entire student body. Father Basil explained life at Holy Cross and informed us of its rules and regulations. He told us to be patient with ourselves, to take one day at a time, and that if we had any problems or questions, not to hesitate to approach him or Father Gregory. Both men came across as very kind and sincere. I would have no hesitation in approaching either of them.

After supper in silence, there was a short indoor recreation period, and night prayers in Latin. Finally, it was time for sleep. When I got to my bed, I quickly took off my clothes, draped them over the chair alongside my bed, and dove under the covers. My parents had bought me pajamas but it hadn't occurred to me to put them on. At home, we never wore pajamas. Suddenly, I noticed the other guys replace their underwear with the pajamas. I felt stupid and embarrassed and as stealthily as possible, took off my shorts and put on my pajamas. I wondered why Pop never told me about this, but then realized I'd never seen Pop in pajamas either. As the lights were turned off, I finally had a moment to myself. It was the first time since I had arrived, that I had a chance to wonder what was happening at home. I also silently hoped that I could adapt to this new life. My friend, Porky, a few beds away, didn't seem worried. He was snoring loud and clear. In a few minutes, I, too, dozed off.

At six the next morning, the whole dorm suddenly came alive with the ear piercing sound of a loud electric bell. We had been warned the night before that we had only fifteen minutes to get dressed, go to the jakes, wash up and be in the chapel for morning prayers. After a week or so, I eventually learned that life at the Prep was controlled by bells. From daybreak until "lights out," every activity began and ended with bells. That first bell in the morning was the most important. There was only one entrance into the chapel and with the whole community present, a late arrival was not an option. There was no such thing as habitual lateness.

One rule that threw us new comers for a loop, was the rule of silence. The silence rule was in full force in the chapel except for vocal prayer. It also ruled in the classroom except for recitation, and it ruled, without exception, in study hall.

We were told that keeping silent would remind us of God's presence. It was a form of self-discipline or what was called "mortification" (another new word). There was always someone who would pull a stunt, especially in study hall, which would cause an outburst of laughter. But if the noise got too loud, it wasn't long before the Vice Prefect would arrive to quiet things down.

Of course, during recreation we all gave our vocal chords a good work-out. We yelled and screamed to our hearts' content. Recreation was a great safety valve, a time to blow off steam. We played hard and took sports seriously. Looking back, I realize now that recreation had served as a real practical part of our training. It stripped away superficiality, the "make-believes" of seminary life. The guys who were able to hit a happy balance of prayer, study, and sports were the ones who persevered. The unbalanced gradually weeded themselves out and eventually quit, or as we said got "shipped home."

When a misfit left or got "shipped" home, it never really surprised me. In fact, I often wondered why it took so long. But what really upset me was when someone I truly admired and thought would make a good priest decided to leave on their own accord. The departure of this type of seminarian was usually "hush hush." An empty seat in the chapel or classroom was the typical way in which we learned of a new departure.

On such occasions, I always tried to figure out what could have been responsible for such a good person's decision to leave.

The first year in Dunkirk slipped by very quickly. I enjoyed seminary life. I was happy, did well in my studies, and made a lot of good friends. The nine months flew by and after final exams, it was time for my first trip home. I was very anxious to get home. When I finally walked in my front door, everything looked so small – the kitchen, the bathroom, and the bedrooms. Mom and Dad gave me a great welcome. My brothers stood around, sized me up and almost seemed lost for words. When we sat down to one of Mom's famous meals, the questions finally started to fly. They asked about the city of Dunkirk and when I described it, they were shocked that it could qualify as a city. They asked about life at Holy Cross and when I described our daily schedule and the rule of silence, my brothers exchanged looks that seemed to say, "Better him than us." They were living in a whole different world than me – cars, jobs, and dates. Harold was a little over ten and nothing I said seemed to interest him. He just wanted to eat and go out to play. Within a week, it was almost as if I'd never left home.

Before leaving for our two month vacation at home, we were given certain guidelines to follow. First, we were told to live and act like seminarians. We were told to visit the parish priests upon arrival home, to go to daily Mass, and at the end of the summer, we each had to get a letter from a parish priest commenting on our conduct. I'm not sure what kind of reception I was expecting at Saint Clare's rectory, but it certainly wasn't a twenty-one gun salute. I was sure the pastor still didn't know my name. He showed little interest in my desire to be a priest. I guess vocations were plentiful in the 1940s and little was done to encourage them on the local level. The local priest barely spoke to me and at the end of the summer, the only comment he could make about my conduct was that I had attended daily Mass.

In some ways, I felt awkward on summer vacation. My aunts and uncles, neighbors, and friends were unusually respectful and on their best behavior around me. I felt like an oddity. They were setting me apart and I didn't like it. Even my old friends watched their words. They often seemed tongue tied around me. I got the feeling that I was viewed as a wet blanket, a killjoy. I felt like saying, "Look, I'm only going on sixteen. Treat me like any other teen. I haven't left the human race." It was difficult.

There were plenty of times that I realized just how similar I was to every other boy my age. Every morning, at the eight o'clock Mass, I saw a very pretty girl that I recognized as a former grade school classmate. Following Mass, she walked home in the same direction as I did. I didn't know whether she recognized me as well, but I did notice glances coming in my direction, too. I often thought about renewing the acquaintance.

The normal attraction was there, but even at that early age, dating or even walking to Mass together would have been considered improper for a seminarian. I wanted the priesthood too much to renew my friendship with this former classmate and so, I never did introduce myself. I simply admired her from afar and kept my "eyes on the prize" of the priesthood.

During this vacation, I also kept myself busy doing odd jobs around the house and in the neighborhood. Actually, I got bored at home and missed the busy routine at Holy Cross. Thank God for one of my uncles who provided a change of pace on the weekends. He had the only car in the family and enjoyed fishing and swimming. I was often chosen as his weekend companion. On Saturdays, he hired a rowboat and we spent the day fishing in Reynolds Channel near Long Beach. On Sunday, we spent the afternoon at Long Beach. I loved the ocean and would spend hours body surfing. I couldn't get enough of it. My uncle, who spent more time on the sand than in the water, had an eye for the girls. His comments about the bathing beauties at Long Beach were funny but usually left me speechless.

Chapter Eight

Just before I returned to Holy Cross on September 10, 1941, my oldest brother Bill got his draft notice. He had to report to New York to board a "troop train" bound for Camp Upton. I remember that day clearly. My mother and I watched as her oldest son left home for the first time. As Bill disappeared to catch a bus, Mom said sadly, "God Bless Billy Boy, may he return safely." A few days later, I left for Dunkirk. The family circle was shrinking.

My first disappointment on returning to the Prep, was realizing the loss of a few of my classmates. I guess the summer vacation took its toll. My friend, Porky Joyce, was one of the dropouts. He joined the Navy a few months later. Stan, a young man from Carnegie, Pennsylvania, joined our second year class as a "new recruit," and would remain a life long friend. I never volunteered as a tour guide for new arrivals. I was too busy swapping summer time stories with my classmates that had returned.

The threat of the United States entering World War II became more apparent each passing day. Hitler was running roughshod over Europe and on December 7, 1941, we crowded around the radio to hear about the attack on Pearl Harbor. The war reached right into the seminary. Priests were called to join the chaplain corps of the Armed Forces. Some of the older fellows left the seminary to enter the Service. There was food rationing, black outs, and gas rationing. Seminarians with brothers in the service were encouraged to send them V-mail letters. Bill, my brother who had been drafted, signed up with the regular Army for four years. He was now sailing to India on the U.S.S. West Point. Ironically, this was the same ship that my brothers Jack and Bill had previously worked to convert into a troop ship back in Robbin's Dry Dock. My brothers, Jack and Bud, also both soon joined the Navy and were off to Newport Naval Base in Rhode Island for boot camp. Strange the way things worked out – Bill who sunburned instantly and hated the beach was stationed in the roaring hot sun of India. Jack, who loved to soak up the sun on the beach, ended up in the freezing waters of the North Atlantic. And Bud, who was always as neat as a pin, spent his Navy career in the jungles of the South Pacific. Four of the Verity boys were now far from home. Only Harold remained home with Mom and Pop.

Dunkirk and the farmland surrounding the Great Lakes were famous for their apple orchards and grape vineyards. With all the young men entering the armed forces, there became a shortage of farm workers and a real possibility of losing the grape harvest. In the spirit of patriotism, classes at Holy Cross were discontinued for the harvest season. After breakfast, we would put on our work clothes, board trucks, and work all day in the Red Wine factory of Fredonia, processing grape juice and jelly. A few of us were selected for the highest paying job at sixty-five cents an hour. Whatever we received in salary went towards our tuition. This was a big help for my parents.

Our job was to stack large, five gallon bottles of hot, pasteurized grape juice in shelves from the floor to the ceiling. It was hard work but we loved it. It beat sitting in class and the study hall pouring over Latin, Greek, French, English, and trigonometry.

Doing the same job in the next bin, separated only by a chicken wire fence, were Italian prisoners of war, under the watchful eyes of Army M.P.s. They were happy, glad to be alive and safely away from the war. At the end of the day's work, they would be loaded onto trucks for their ride back to the prison camp, while we were loaded onto trucks for our ride back to Holy Cross. The whole experience was a positive one. We helped the war effort and welcomed the change of pace. We even managed to have a lot of fun. Pat Crowe from Pittsburgh, "Bush" Kissane, and I had so much fun that our practical jokes and laughter even made the POW's laugh.

Of course, this period was also a stressful one for me. With three service stars hanging in the front window at home, three brothers overseas, and word trickling back to the seminary about friends and neighbors being wounded or killed, I was convinced I should enter the Service. I was seventeen and ready to go. In my heart, I was convinced that I would be a better priest for the experience. I had many an open heart discussion with a kind and understanding priest at the seminary. He said the choice would have to be mine but he reminded me that the door of Holy Cross swung only one way and that if I chose to leave I would not be reaccepted. I gave it a lot of thought, said some extra prayers, and remained in the Prep. By the time I completed the six years in Dunkirk, I was the only one remaining from the original class of twelve.

Chapter Nine

Leaving Holy Cross for the Novitiate in Pittsburgh was like leaving a farm team for the major leagues. It was serious business, a solid year in basic training for the religious life. Between Holy Cross and the novitiate, I had three weeks vacation at home. It was my shortest vacation, but by far the best. Mom and Pop were thrilled to have their five sons back home again. My three older brothers had all returned safely from the War and were in Uncle Sam's 52-20 Club. They spent the summer relaxing, putting on weight, and in no rush to get jobs. Twenty dollars a week from Uncle Sam was enough to pay for gas to get to the beach and some trips to the local bars. Since I was going on twenty-one, the age gap between my brothers and I no longer seemed so great. There were lots of jokes, laughter, war stories, and just plain old fun. After dinner, we'd all just sit around talking and enjoying each others' company. Even Harold, who was only fifteen and had never before shown any interest in the adult conversation, hung around until Pop donned the apron and started to sing.

The three weeks passed quickly. It wasn't all beach and fun. There were family visits and tear-filled goodbyes with relatives and friends. There were trips to Jamaica to buy an all black outfit – suit, shoes, tie, overcoat and even a black fedora. When I tried the outfit on for the first time, my brother Jack said I looked like "Digby the Undertaker." In the third week of July, Mom, Pop, my four brothers, relatives, and friends gave me a grand send-off at LaGuardia Airport. Within a few hours of take-off, I would be in the Novitiate in Pittsburgh – the point of no return.

I heard a lot of exaggerated, horror stories about life in the Novitiate – the strict silence, the shaved heads, the bread and coffee breakfast, and most of all, the chanting of the divine office from two to three o'clock every morning. It sounded like a religious form of boot camp where the men were separated from the boys. If I had any doubts about my calling to the religious life, a year in the Novitiate would settle them. I knew the year in Pittsburgh would be serious business, but I also knew that the previous six year stint in Dunkirk hadn't exactly been a picnic.

I was named Dean of my new class at the Novitiate. This distinction was not based on holiness, intelligence, or leadership ability. It was based on seniority and mine dated back to my freshman year in Holy Cross. I was the sole survivor of that original class. The greatest asset of being Dean, or class representative, was that I had daily contact with the Master of Novices, Father Berchman Lanigan. I saw Father Berchman on his good days and his bad days. If he got upset or angry, I didn't get flustered because he was a very fair man and I knew his reprimands were well deserved, whether directed at me or my classmates. Because I was able to remain calm during his "storms," Father Lanigan nicknamed me "The Excitable Dean." It go so, that when the entire class was present, he would take a puff on his cigar, give out new assignments, chuckle and good naturedly say, "Now, don't get excited, Dean." When the Master chuckled, the entire class laughed, including me. A good laugh, for whatever reason, was always welcomed in those days.

August 14, 1946, was Vestition Day on which we were clothed in a modified Passionist habit and sandals, and our heads were shaved down to the bone. We were given copies of the Passionist Rule and Regulations, which would fashion our religious lives. From this day on, we were officially made novices and we could no longer use our Baptismal names. I was no longer Gerard. Instead, I was now Gordon. This symbolized a complete turn-over, a new leaf, and a fresh start in the religious life.

During recreation, we started to make up nicknames based on our new names. I became known as "Flash Gordon" after the comic strip hero. This nickname soon became "Fresh" Gordon and eventually "Flush Gordon." Bathroom humor was highly appreciated in those days. About eleven months later, the Master asked me if I was happy. I honestly was happy and told him so. He then asked if I liked the name "Gordon." To remain honest, I admitted that I wasn't crazy about it. When he asked why, I responded, "After much research, I couldn't find a Saint Gordon and I don't expect to be the first." The master paused and said that starting on the day of Profession, August 15, 1947, I would be renamed "James" – the first apostle to be martyred. This made me very happy.

Father Berchman, or as we secretly called him, "Berky," knew the Passionist Rule and Religious Life inside and out. His daily conferences and instructions were crystal clear. His conferences were a complete change of pace from the classroom atmosphere at Holy Cross. He had terrific insights into human nature and God help anyone foolish enough to try to bluff him. He had no patience for any kind of deviousness. He was straight forward and expected the novices to be just as up front with him. He led by example.

On Profession Day, my parents and four brothers came to Pittsburgh to see me clothed in the Passionist habit and hear me publicly pronounce my vows. It was another step closer to my ultimate goal of becoming a Passionist priest. The year in the Novitiate was the happiest, most peaceful, and most spiritual time of my life. I was ready to take on philosophy and theology

– six more years in the classroom before ordination into the priesthood.

I was also ready to live up to the four vows just professed as a Passionist: poverty, chastity, obedience, and the unique fourth vow which singled out the Passionists from all other religious communities – to promote devotion to the Passion of Jesus Christ in the hearts of the faithful. I took these vows without any hesitation or reservation.

I found the vow of poverty the easiest of the vows to accept. Poverty was designed to free me from all cares and worries that come from ownership of material goods. Being detached from worldly goods was supposed to ease me in my search for God. Practicing religious poverty was not meant to be an end in itself.

Actually, moving into a tiny room, or monastic cell, with only a small table, wooden chair and a straw mattress on wooden planks was not a big sacrifice. Up to this point, I had never had a private room, either at home or in the seminary. After spending six years in a dormitory, a monastic cell was a treat. In the winter, I had heat. In the summer, there was a window to open. The world is crowded with good people far more impoverished than those with a vow of poverty. A truly poor person would have considered my lifestyle a luxury. There was no comparison between my living conditions and those of the poor in crowded tenements or the homeless in the streets.

People from the middle and upper classes might have thought that having no spending money in my pocket or car in the garage was a great sacrifice. It wasn't. Remembering the generosity of my parents and the personal sacrifices they made so that I could attend the seminary, served as a constant reminder of my good fortune. Their generosity made my life in religion possible. I always felt my life would be a sham or parasitical if I ever forgot for one minute, those who made my search for God possible.

As for the vow of chastity, I knew it would be no easy task. I never really lived on a "cloud" or in denial. I was able to keep my feet planted firmly on earth. As a matter of fact, I had a million reminders that I walked with feet of clay. There was nothing special about me. I had the same flesh and blood as my brothers, the same natural instincts. Whether it was in school, in church, or on the beach, I always appreciated the manner in which God designed the opposite sex. Like one little child said, "God doesn't make junk." And I wholeheartedly agreed.

To look upon every woman as a personal threat to salvation would be the working of a warped, sick mind. Such an attitude wouldn't say much for the Creator's handiwork. I witnessed the lifelong, mutual love my parents had for each other, the joys and sacrifices of their love, and the satisfaction they received from raising the children that God gave them. I took the vow of chastity with my eyes wide open – it would be difficult, but it would also enable me to choose a way of life with less distraction. I could be more focused in devoting myself, my time, and my energy to doing God's work.

Some of the most unhappy people in the world are probably celibates who forget how to love. There can be no selfishness in chastity – it thrives by loving God, by loving God in our neighbor, and by loving our neighbor in God. Chastity that becomes self-serving and is no longer inflamed with love becomes sterility. Chastity is like a candle which gets its prominence and enhances its own worth only when it is ignited and fuels the flames of love. If the flame of love flickers and dies, the candle of chastity serves no purpose.

The vow of obedience was a solemn promise to live my life according to the Passionist Rule and to follow the commands of my lawful religious superiors in all that is good and holy. In the seven years preceding my vows, I never thought of myself as an indecisive robot following the whims and fancies of an unreasonable or tyrannical superior. Based on past experiences in following the direction given by prudent superiors, I couldn't foresee any reason for not taking the vow of obedience. When Saint Benedict, the founder of the Benedictines, was asked what quality was most desirable for a religious superior, he responded, "If a monk is holy, let him pray for us. If a monk is learned, let him teach us. If a monk is prudent, choose him to lead us." Choosing the wrong person as a superior, could turn religious life into a nightmare. An egotistical superior who thinks he is endowed with infallibility can blot out all initiative and creativity on the part of the community. An arrogant leader who looks upon any form of delegation as a diminution of his capability and leadership, can easily squelch community involvement and end up with a one-man show. A religious superior needs his community more than his community needs him.

I don't know how much merit there was in following orders that were reasonable. Most people, no matter the profession, do this every day. My father, the fireman, without a vow of obedience, had to respond instantaneously to every alarm that sounded. He never hesitated to follow an order to rush into a burning building – risking his own life for someone else's.

As a religious, I might not have jumped for joy at every directive given me, but my obedience certainly never rose to the level of heroic. Any personal thoughts of heroism in pronouncing my religious vows would quickly evaporate when I compared them to the hardship my parents endured in faithfully embracing their own versions of poverty, chastity, and obedience.

The fourth vow I took on August 15, 1947 is a unique vow which sets the Passionist apart from all other religious groups. It is a vow to develop devotion to the Passion of Jesus, first in one's personal life and then, to promote this devotion in the hearts of others. Keeping this vow was not merely a case of preaching or telling the story of Calvary on television or radio, or in books. The Passionist lay brother, who never preached a sermon is his life, can be more effective in promoting devotion to Christ's Passion than the most persuasive preacher.

A modern Passionist would have to be living in a bubble not to be aware of the suffering in the world – poverty, hunger, homelessness and sickness. A Passionist who knows how suffering was sanctified on Calvary, can not make the Cross disappear. But, he can help teach the sufferers of the redemptive value of bearing their own Cross. To seek suffering for its own sake would be irrational, but to waste the inevitable suffering that comes into our lives would be tragic. The lonely senior, the confused teen, the AIDS victim, and the countless others, are reaching out to someone who can teach them how to bear the Cross pressing on their shoulders. The Passionist has been called to help.

I took these four vows without reservation. I was happy and proud to be a Passionist. It was time to move on and complete my training for the priesthood.

Chapter Ten

For the next six years as a Passionist student, I would follow the full monastic schedule. This meant beginning the day by chanting the Divine Office at two in the morning, attending Mass, having a quick breakfast of bread and coffee, and taking a silent solitary walk. It was a contemplative form of life.

For the remainder of the day, the bulk of my time was spent in class, private study and prayer, and an evening solitary walk. There were two half hour recreation periods following lunch and supper. Aside from the recreation periods, silence was observed. This was my lifestyle as I advanced from two years of philosophy into four years of theology. The six years of study were divided into three years in Massachusetts, two in Maryland, and the final year in Union City, New Jersey.

Thirteen years, preparing for the priesthood, is a long time. On my first day in Dunkirk, I had eleven classmates. Over the course of a few years, the original eleven, for various reasons, departed. Of the twenty or so who joined subsequently, only eleven remained and so, once again, I was in a class of twelve.

Is there such a thing as a temporary calling? I think there is. I've spoken to many former seminarians and they never considered their temporary stay in the seminary as a waste of time. The spiritual impact of the seminary or religious life is a profound one and can exert a very positive influence in places where priests and religious are not found.

Each evening before supper, a half hour was set aside for a solitary walk around the monastery grounds. I loved the combination of fresh air, some exercise, and an opportunity for some self-reflection and private thought. After a day of non-stop community prayers, study, class lectures and more study, the walk was relaxing and a time for enjoying the luxury of creative thinking. The walks I enjoyed most were the ones I took while at Saint Gabriel's Monastery in Brighton, a suburb of Boston.

Saint Gabriel's Monastery was perched on a hill that overlooked the Boston skyline. I especially enjoyed walking in the dark, crisp fall air. Looking down from the hill, it seemed as though there were a million pinpoints of light reaching up from homes, hospitals, and office buildings. I began to wonder about all the people behind those lights, especially the patients in all those lighted rooms in the Marine Hospital. I thought a lot about those patients.

As I strolled comfortably on the hill above, I couldn't help but think about the pain, the sickness and the loneliness being endured by the patients a short distance away. We were so close physically and yet worlds apart. I used to ask myself, "How come I, a twenty-two year old Passionist, never had a serious sick day in my life?" Why was I so fortunate and they so sick? I know I prayed for them and thanked God for my blessings, but wondered why I would have to wait to become a priest before I could help them.

After giving it a lot of thought, I asked my classmates if they would like to join me in visiting the patients down the hill. I realized that my suggestion was a break in tradition but, as I remember it, my classmates were very agreeable. A short time later, the Provincial Superior came to Saint Gabriel's for his annual visitation, which gave him the opportunity to speak privately with each member of the monastery.

During my turn with the Provincial, I requested permission for my classmates and myself to assist the chaplain of the Marine Hospital in visiting the patients. He was totally unprepared for this, looked at me like I had two heads, and was genuinely shocked that I would suggest such a thing. There was no room for discussion. Without any hesitation he said, "No," and his reason was, "You'll all be falling in love with the nurses."

The Provincial's reaction was quite a blow. He threw cold water on what I thought would be a great apostolate, an opportunity to comfort the sick, the lonely, and the dying. Falling in love with a nurse might have been a possibility, but it had never crossed my mind. The words of Jesus, "Whatever you do unto the least of my brothers, you do unto me," suddenly made a lot more sense. The Provincial's reasoning was a bitter pill to swallow, but being an obedient religious, swallow I did. I still felt like a religious glutton on the hill, devouring all kind of spiritual goodies and not allowed to share them with my less fortunate neighbors below. I was hankering for some kind of spiritual outlet. The priesthood couldn't come fast enough.

In the meantime, great spiritual men like Fathers Berchman and Theodore Foley helped me to deepen my faith and realize that, in some mysterious way, all of our lives are somehow intertwined. The sick man lying in a hospital bed and the man on his knees in a monastery chapel - one in pain and the other in prayer - each seeking separately to do God's will and both bringing God closer.

Chapter Eleven

Finally, after thirteen years of preparation, the day for Ordination to the Priesthood arrived. It was the feast of Saint Gabriel, February 27, 1953. Our Ordination took place in Saint Michael's Church in Union City. The long awaited day of Ordination is a very solemn, holy, and happy day for both the ordained and for the families that made it possible.

The most solemn part of the ceremony is when the candidates for the priesthood are summoned to kneel before the ordaining bishop for the imposition of his hands on the heads of the "ordinandi." The twelve of us lined up, and, two by two, we would kneel before the bishop. Following the Passionist custom, we were supposed to approach in dean order. My classmate, Father Stan, and I knelt down first. The bishop was about to impose his hand on Stan first. Stan shook his head and with his folded hands, pointed to me. The bishop smiled, and ordained me first. Stan, my classmate of twelve years, on his first day as a priest, instructed Bishop Boland how to observe dean order. After the ceremony, Stan and I had a good laugh about it.

At the conclusion of the ceremony, the parents of the new priests kneel down at the altar rail to receive the blessings of their sons, now priests. When I went to bless my parents, my Mom was so excited that I thought she was going to jump over the rail. Pop knelt with his head bowed. I was both happy and humbled by these two great people who brought me into the world twenty-seven years before. They were kneeling and asking me for my blessing, when I felt I should be kneeling and asking them for their blessing.

On our way home, my mother asked if we could stop at Calvary Cemetery to bless her parents' graves. It took some time for the reality of the priesthood to settle in, but the graveside prayers certainly helped me realize that I was finally a priest. The next day, I visited my father's mother who was bedridden. I said Mass for her and the immediate family in her little apartment overlooking Hillside Avenue in Jamaica. This quiet Mass for my bedridden grandmother brought a great deal of joy to her and her children, all of whom encircled her bed. This was far more rewarding for me than all the fanfare and excitement that was to follow a few days later in my boyhood parish of Saint Clare's.

My first solemn Mass in Saint Clare's was like a walk down memory lane. The little altar boys reminded me of the many dark, cold winter mornings that I jumped out of bed and rushed to be on time to serve Mass. I made a promise to myself that day. I promised that I would always find time after Mass to thank these little unsung heroes for their generous service. There in the sanctuary to assist me in celebrating the solemn Mass, were the two Passionists who welcomed me into Holy Cross thirteen years before – Fathers Basil and Gregory.

Out in the pews, beside my parents, brothers, and relatives, were neighbors, customers from my paper route, and even some of my curbside companions. All of them were there to greet me, ask for blessings, and wish me well. It was a great reunion – a day of joy and thanksgiving. After a few days of quiet at home, it was back to Union City, as a newly ordained priest, to join my classmates in completing our final year of theology.

Because the primary mission of Passionists is to preach parish missions and to conduct spiritual retreats, every newly ordained, without exception, had to successfully complete a full year of homiletics – sermon writing and delivery. A complete portfolio of mission and retreat sermons had to be written and approved. In addition to the composition of sermons, each one of us had to give practice sermons before our classmates and instructor. I found these practice sermons very difficult, and the critiques that followed were very deflating. Thank God for the opportunity each weekend to preach before a live audience in a parish setting. This was a long year and I can't remember how many times I must have said, "Dear God, when will this ever end?"

During this final year of training, my dream of seven years was finally realized. I was asked to cover for the chaplain in Mercy Hospital in downtown Springfield, Massachusetts. I jumped at this opportunity to do hands on chaplain's work. The Sisters, nurses and doctors were all very kind to me. It must have been very apparent that I was an "eager beaver" rookie chaplain.

My first night in the chaplain quarters was a restless one. In the middle of the night, I got a phone call to report to the Emergency Room. I rushed down and administered the Last Rites to a woman who died in the ambulance enroute to Mercy. The next morning, I had to report the night's activities to the hospital's record keeping department. When asked for the report, I said, "I had one D.O.D." The women in the office looked up from their desks and one asked, "What's D.O.D.?" I answered, "Dead on Delivery." All the women laughed and one said, "Father, it's D.O.A. – Dead on Arrival." The young hot shot chaplain had a lot to learn.

In June of 1954, our basic training for the mission was completed. Rumors were hot and heavy. The twelve of us were assembled for our assignments. The class was split down the middle. Six of us were told to pack our bags and report to Saint

Gabriel's in Toronto, Canada. The other six were sent to Rome, Catholic University, and elsewhere for additional studies. While Rome would have been a great experience, a couple of more years in the classroom would have been a terrible price to pay. Saint Gabriel's in Toronto was a new monastery with a young, active staff. There was a great demand for all kinds of priestly work – it was an answer to my prayer.

We weren't in Toronto very long when we were told that the Cenacle Retreat House was requesting a priest to conduct a high school senior retreat. I volunteered for the assignment. I was anxious to get my feet wet. The retreat was successful and the Cenacle Sisters invited me back for more retreats. I enjoyed working with teens and apparently the kids spread the word. Youth retreats almost became a full time apostolate.

After a short time in youth retreat work, I received a phone call from very distraught parents. Their daughter had been admitted to a psychiatric hospital for attempting suicide. The disturbed teen refused to talk to her parents or doctor. She told her parents that she would only talk to a Father James who had conducted her retreat. The parents located me and asked me to visit their daughter.

When I entered her hospital room, I did not recognize the teen with the bandaged wrists. She obviously remembered me from the retreat and was very happy that I came to see her. We

had a good talk, said a few prayers, and before leaving, I told
her I would return the following day.

She said, "If I tell you a secret, can I trust you?" She reached
under her mattress and pulled out a large sharp sliver of china
from a dish she had smashed earlier. She put me to the test
and said if I didn't report it, she would not cut herself with it. I
promised to keep her secret, but in turn, she had to promise to
turn over the sliver to me the next day.

I had a sleepless night and must have said a million prayers
for the troubled kid. Thankfully, the next day, she gave me a big
smile when I entered her room. I kept my half of the bargain
and she kept hers. She also shared her problem. She loved
her parents but said they weren't good listeners and wouldn't
understand anyway. I asked her to have faith in her parents and
to talk it all out with her doctor.

I gave her my blessing, put the sliver of china in my pocket
and breathed a big sigh of relief as I got on the elevator. About
six weeks later, her parents invited me to a welcome home
party for their talkative daughter.

In spite of my inexperience in the retreat ministry, God
found a way to help this fragile teen. The fact that God used
me as an instrument of grace for that teen is proof positive of
"how God can write straight on crooked lines."

Chapter Twelve

After fifteen years of being stationed out of town, I was finally transferred from Toronto to Immaculate Conception Monastery in Jamaica, New York. Mom, Pop, and the entire family were delighted to have me back on Long Island. I was called upon to officiate at marriages, baptize nephews and nieces, and to bury a number of relatives and friends.

Occasionally, I could get home to have a quiet meal with Mom and Pop, or even participate in some of the larger family gatherings on special occasions. Going home was no longer a major production. A short walk to a city bus, less than a dollar fare, and a twenty minute ride would bring me home to Mom and Pop. It was 1955 and it was the first time since 1940 that the five "Verity boys" were back on Long Island.

The Jamaica Monastery looked like a mighty fortress perched high on a hill overlooking busy Hillside Avenue below. Attached to the Monastery, were an active retreat house and a vibrant parish church. The whole complex was a beehive of spiritual activity. There was a constant flow of laymen, priests, and religious coming to the monastery and retreat house for confession and spiritual direction. Because of the large religious community present, the liturgy in the parish church was outstanding and attracted many visitors from all over Queens County.

It was a holy place that attracted a steady stream of pilgrims. The monastic setting, the liturgy and Gregorian chant, along with the availability of priests for confessions and spiritual guidance, attracted men and women from all walks of life, both saints and sinners. The steep climb from the bus stops on Hillside Avenue or the subway below was a small price to pay for the peace that was to be found on the hilltop.

Jamaica Monastery was an exciting and inspirational place for a young priest. The monastic life of the Passionists was a blending of contemplation and activity, as envisioned by the Founder, Saint Paul of the Cross. It was a great place to participate in the ministry in all of its fullness – sharing in the prayer of the community in preparation for a challenging apostolate.

One change of pace from the monastic routine was "Sunday work." Each Saturday morning, a list of parishes requiring help for Saturday confessions and Sunday Mass was posted. Those not conducting missions or retreats would be assigned to this "Sunday work." I enjoyed meeting the local priests, hearing confessions, and I welcomed the opportunity to preach. The only thing I found missing in a number of rectories, was the lack of priestly companionship – the camaraderie I had enjoyed in the monastery. In some rectories, after Saturday night supper, each priest would quietly drift off to his own suite of rooms. Life in a rectory, without a family spirit, could be a very lonely existence.

As a young priest, I was happy and proud to dress up and wear my black suit and Roman collar. For the most part, in major cities like New York, Boston, and Philadelphia, people of all faith were courteous and respectful towards me. As a healthy young priest, I was often embarrassed on a crowded subway when older people would get up and offer me their seats. Sometimes parents would nudge their children and tell them to give the "Father" their seat. I always gratefully acknowledged the kind gesture, looked for a reason to remain standing, and used the occasion to strike up a conversation.

I had a rude awakening one windy, bitter cold Saturday afternoon. I had just gotten off the "El" in Williamsburg, Brooklyn. As I walked down Marcy Avenue on the way to Transfiguration Parish, I had to hold onto my black fedora to keep it from blowing away. Coming towards me on the same side of the street were four men dressed very much like me – all in black, including their fedoras. As they grew close, I looked up to greet them.

When my Roman collar became visible, they stopped in their tracks. I heard their angry mutters, although I could not make out their words. Suddenly, they cleared their throats and with great contempt, spit on the sidewalk at my feet. These Hassidic Jews looked as though they were filled with hatred and quickly changed their direction, continuing to mutter as they crossed the street. It was as if they had confronted the devil himself.

I was totally flabbergasted as I watched them quickly move down the other side of the street. They were nothing like my little Jewish friends that I shared my childhood with. They were nothing like the Jewish parents of friends who invited me into their homes and were happy to have me as a playmate of their sons. A short time after this incident, I asked a Jewish friend what I might have done to provoke such a reaction. He told me it wasn't what I did, but what I represented. He said, as a Jew, that he was embarrassed by their misconduct. He said that some Hassidic Jews were known for their fanaticism and intolerance and asked me not to tar all Jews with the same brush. I told him I wouldn't tar him with the same brush as long as he wouldn't lump me together with the intolerant Christians who think they own God.

One lesson I learned that day was that I should never expect the Roman collar to be a passport to special treatment. Any respect I received as a priest, needed to be earned. The collar does not make the priest; the priest makes the collar.

Chapter Thirteen

I'll never forget the mixture of joy and fear that I experienced as I opened the letter from the Mission Office which assigned me to my first parish mission. I was to accompany a very seasoned missionary to the English parish of Saint Aloysius in Montreal, for two weeks. The primary apostolate of the Passionist was the preaching of parish missions. All the study and the years of training were finally paying off. I was determined to do my best.

My main concern was that my best wouldn't be good enough. To be evaluated by one of our most talented, experienced missionaries, was rather intimidating. He could hold the entire congregation spellbound. He could loosen up the parishioners with some introductory humor and a few minutes later, terrify them with the threat of punishment for their sins. From the back of the church, I listened to his message, observed his presentation, and watched the reaction of people in the pews. Some of the laity were so pleased they couldn't wait to encourage their friends to join them the following night. Others quietly disappeared. In any case, he was a tough act to follow.

On the second night, it was my turn to preach. I was frightened, nervous, and very jittery. I felt like the future of my missionary career hinged on my presentation that night. The sermon content, its delivery, and the reaction of the congregation were all being evaluated. Would I go blank or stutter? Would my delivery be as flat as a pancake?

When I ascended the mission platform in the sanctuary and stood alongside of the large crucifix, there was absolute silence. The church was full, wall to wall people. I took a deep breath and made a few wobbly remarks. But when I finally made eye contact with the congregation, I saw very kind, sympathetic and encouraging faces. These parishioners sensed both my inexperience and my sincere desire to help them. Their reaction was electric. I was quickly able to forget myself and concentrate on my message to a church filled with wonderful people.

I still had a lot to learn and much to do to improve my missionary technique. In all of my early mission assignments, I was very fortunate to share the preaching with seasoned missionaries. For the most part, they were good, kind, and compassionate priests. What became apparent, was that the more a missionary scolded, screamed, or preached fire and brimstone, the shorter the lines at his confessional became. I often thought it ironic that those who preached hell and fire, always managed to finish confessions early enough on Saturday night to get home in time to catch "Gunsmoke" on TV!

For me, the benchmark of a successful parish mission was neither the eloquence of the missionary or the crowded church. It was not the people sitting in the pews but the number of people on their knees in the confessionals. If ever there was a time for a priest to radiate the mercy of Jesus, it was in the confessional. Passionists, for the most part, had the reputation as good, kind, and understanding confessors. Confession wasn't a time for scolding the penitent or for handing out their penances according to some mathematical equation. It was a time for gently helping the penitent to find the peace that comes from seeking God's forgiveness. What took place in the secrecy of the confessional was the hallmark of a successful mission. Whoever was responsible for letting this great Sacrament fall into desuetude has a lot of explaining to do.

I had the good fortune to preach many parish missions throughout the Northeast. But the highlight of my mission career took place in Saint Peter's Parish in Rome, New York. It was a citywide mission specifically organized for teens. Teenagers from all the neighboring parishes were invited to Saint Peter's.

Teenagers are an earthly lot. It's very hard for them to relate to an invisible God. To tell them that God is as present to them as the air they breathe, doesn't really cut it. To tell them God is kind and forgiving and that their sins are no match for divine mercy, is unconvincing. An abstract God is distant and impersonal.

A teen congregation is also very demanding, highly critical, and frighteningly perceptive. Their evaluation of the preacher is almost spontaneous. The politeness of an adult congregation can lull a preacher into a false sense of security and complacency. Bored adults sit quietly, stifle yawns and perhaps sneak looks at their watches. Bored teens will vocalize their yawns, and will even shake their wrist watches to make sure they're still working. They will whisper, giggle, and occasionally even get up and walk out.

A priest with an audience of teens has to be patient, understanding, and empathetic. He has to be able to climb inside the teenager, to understand where the young person is coming from. If the silly antics of a few teens in the church can get under the preacher's skin, and he singles them out for a scolding, he succeeds only in alienating his young congregation. He becomes just another cranky adult who is down on kids!

On the second night of the Saint Peter's mission, before getting into the sermons, I asked the young congregation, "How are you making out?" They got a startled look on their faces and laughter erupted throughout the church. I realized as soon as the words escaped my mouth that I had chosen my words poorly. I felt my face flush and turn all colors of the rainbow. I quickly explained that what I really meant to ask was, "How are you doing?" They laughed a little more, relaxed, settled down, and *listened*. Their attendance didn't slacken off; there was actually a standing room only. I thanked them for their attendance.

No one can introduce God to a teen better than another teen. If they feel at home in "God's house," then God's house becomes their house. When they are comfortable, they listen. And when they are inspired, they can't wait to share their joy with their peers.

Hearing confessions hours on end can be exhausting. Sitting in a dark, cramped, poorly ventilated confessional makes it very difficult to stay awake. One afternoon when I finished some "after school" confessions, I dashed out to the front steps of Saint Peter's for a breath of fresh air. I wasn't out there long when a woman approached me. She said I looked exhausted and offered to help me "unwind." She made it very obvious what her intentions were. I was startled, almost speechless. The only response I could muster was, "No thanks."

She gave me a weak little smile that seemed to say, "Oh well, I tried to help." As she walked down the steps of Saint Peter's and headed up the street, I felt sad. I wasn't angry or annoyed with her, but I was disappointed in the way I handled the situation. Was there something I could have done or said that would have helped this poor woman?

I remembered the story of Jesus resting by a well when he met the Samaritan woman. He was gentle and kind with the poor adulterous woman. I just hope my, "No thanks," wasn't interpreted as abhorrence or disdain. Maybe I should have thanked God for making my humanity so obvious as to make me approachable. Is it a stretch to think that God looked beyond the humanity of this lady and saw only her kindness in trying to help another human in the only way she knew how? Who is to judge?

The clincher of that teen mission was Friday night. On this night, standing alongside a large crucifix, I would ask the teenagers to put all distracting thoughts out of their minds and to join with me in trying to create a mental picture of the suffering and execution of Jesus on Calvary. "Crucifixion" was a holy word, not familiar to teens. "Execution" was familiar and graphic, something they could grasp.

As I described Jesus' agony in the garden and his anticipation of his own execution, I could see the teens relating to his fear. In Jesus' trial before Pilate, they understood what it was to be ridiculed and shouted down. They knew how much false accusations could hurt and how peer pressures could sway.

Young people were really puzzled by the horrible execution of Jesus. For them, it was mind boggling that anyone could kill a person who fed the hungry, defended the children, gave sight to the blind, and healed the sick. The full impact of Jesus' sacrifice hit home when the young congregation realized that Jesus, as God's son, went through all of this for them. It dawned on them that there was only one answer to the question, "Were you there when they crucified my Lord?" The answer was, "Yes, I was there."

At the end of the service, there was no mad stampede to leave the church. A number of the teens left the pews to kneel before the crucifix. Extra priests were called in to accommodate all those who wanted to go to confession. Teens found a God to whom they could relate – a God who could sweat, feel abandoned, be falsely accused, and shed blood. They wanted to share their problems with a God that would understand.

Those, especially clergymen, who scoff at a sermon on the Passion and death of Jesus, as pure history or as a sheer emotional appeal, are out of touch with their sense saturated congregation. In the real world, we hear the cursing, the blasphemy, and the perjury. We see the cruelty, the bloodshed, the violence, and the executions of the innocent. From the crib to the Cross, we can relate to the human nature of Jesus.

Our youth, so filled with life and far from death, can find it difficult to relate to the resurrected Jesus, the second person of the Holy Trinity. Young Christians are naturally and spiritually energetic – they want to save the world. They have the energy to imitate Jesus in the performance of the corporal works of mercy. Later in life, when they run out of steam, and begin to slow down, their thoughts and prayers will turn more heavenward to the resurrected Jesus.

A teen mission I gave in Saint Benedict's Parish in Richmond Hill was a study in contrasts between the holiness of the old and the young. The pastor who hosted the mission was a real, priestly gentleman. He was the superintendent of all the Catholic schools in the Brooklyn Diocese. He set high scholastic standards for the thousands of teens in Catholic schools, as well as strict codes of conduct, both of which the religious Sisters and Brothers enforced.

To his credit, this pastor who spent a large part of his priesthood fostering Catholic education, was very concerned about the majority of his young parishioners who attended public schools. One would think that of all the pastors in the Brooklyn Diocese, he who spent so much time in the elite parochial school system, would be the least inclined to have a teen mission for public school kids. Here, was the sedate pastor, opening the church door to the most rambunctious of all of his parishioners.

The mission was to begin Sunday night. A half hour before the mission was to begin, the streets were empty. Ten minutes before starting time, the block outside was swarming with teens. When the church doors were opened, the youthful congregation made a mad scramble for the seats. The noise, the chatter, and the laughter were ear shattering. The old pastor, in his monsignor robes, stood in the center aisle and tried to bring order out of chaos. His efforts in appealing for silence went unheeded. I wouldn't have blamed him if he had second thoughts about such a venture. He came into the sacristy red faced and said, "I give up. They're all yours."

Each night, he was outside the church, greeting his young parishioners. Each night, the crowd became more subdued. During the service, the pastor would open the sacristy door a crack, listen to my sermon and marvel at the sustained attendance throughout the week. He was all smiles as he watched the increasing number of teens going to the sacrament each night.

At the close of the mission on Friday night, he had nothing but praise for his energetic congregation. His young flock radiated holiness and so did their Good Shepherd, each in their own way.

Sadly, our congregations today are looking more and more like a mixture of day care centers and senior citizen clubs - the very young, a few in between, and the very old. The young vibrant crowds, my previous hope for the future, are now our dropouts. The hundreds of thousands of young people who turn out for the Pope's Youth Days are the hand picked parishioners, not the parish drop-outs. The greatest sin of omission the clergy commit these days is their failure to seek out and harvest the energy and idealism of the forgotten youth in the congregation.

Chapter Fourteen

In the mid fifties, the Passionists joined the national trend in vocational recruiting. It was a time of expansion and growth for dioceses and religious communities. New parishes, schools, hospitals, and mission fields had to be staffed. With an eye to the future, a whole new emphasis on seeking candidates for the priesthood emerged. Eye catching vocational literature and posters became plentiful. Most vocational directors had a healthy supply of handouts, slides, and films. They were poised and ever ready at a moment's notice to participate in vocational rallies, visit high schools and college campuses.

Unlike other parish priests or religious communities involved in teaching youth, the Passionists lacked visibility. The fact that Passionists were considered an austere monastic community, that blended contemplation with mission activity, put them at a disadvantage. Similar to the Marines, the challenging lifestyle of the Passionists had a limited mass appeal. But I believed that as long as the Passionist vocational directors painted a true picture, not a watered down version, there would always be some candidates ready to accept the challenge.

I was assigned to be the local vocational director of Jamaica, responsible for recruiting throughout Long Island, New York City, and the adjoining counties of the New York Archdiocese. Vocational work was slowly becoming a full time job – forming a vocational club, visiting schools, participating in rallies, and taking prospective candidates on weekend tours of Holy Cross. Once a young man expressed the desire to be a Passionist and was judged qualified, the follow-up work would begin. There would be home visits to meet the candidate's parents, reference checks, parish approvals, medical exams, etc. Finally, once the applicant's file was completed, it would be forwarded to the seminary or novitiate for final acceptance.

As the workload increased, the young, enthusiastic Passionist seminarians and Brothers in the Jamaica Monastery came to my assistance. They helped run the Vocational meetings and manned the booths at the local vocational exhibits. Their friendly, smiling faces did more to attract vocations than all of our literature, films, and slide presentations put together. More and more, future Passionists were appearing from the New York area.

When the Chinese communists expelled the American Passionists from the Hunan Province, my boyhood dreams of becoming a foreign missionary were all but completely dashed.

It was during my vocational works that the Passionists decided to open a new mission in the southern Philippines on the Island of Mindanao. New missionaries were being recruited. I immediately approached the Provincial and volunteered for the assignment. He sugar coated his refusal by telling me that he was very aware of my success in youth work and planned to assign me as Father Ronald's replacement as the General Vocational Director. Ronald not only served as a missionary in China, but now received a second chance to serve in the Philippines. Meanwhile, I was about to be buried under an ever growing mound of paper work in Jamaica. Ronald got the job I always dreamed of, and I got the job he was happy to give up. So be it.

Ronald had a secretary. I had none. He had a station wagon. I needed one. There was a lot to be done with almost no time to make the transition. Thankfully, Father Felix, the rector of the Jamaica Monastery, built me an office and meeting room in the basement. The pastor of the monastery parish was able to send me a group of women to serve as volunteer secretaries.

The time, effort, and man power that the Passionists put into vocational work was one of the greatest investments they made in their own future. One day, while I was in the vocational office, I received a call from a young lady named Patricia. She said she was thinking about becoming a Dominican Sister and was advised by Sister Geraldine of New Jersey to get in touch with me. Apparently, a Passionist in Toronto suggested that Sister Geraldine send Patricia to me for vocational guidance. Of course, I told Patricia that I would be happy to see her and help her in any way that I could.

This reminded me of the time that I, as a teenager, told Father Rath of Saint Boniface that I was interested in being a missionary. His suggestion that I talk to a missionary who was to visit the parish the following week was an important one. That missionary, a stranger, set in motion a succession of events that led to my ordination thirteen years later.

Isn't it mysterious how total strangers can walk into our lives and somehow begin a chain of events that can impact us for years to come? When strangers freely meet in the search of truth or the pursuit of goodness, how can God not have a part in such an encounter?

Understandably, Patricia was frightened by the prospect of visiting the Passionist Monastery in Jamaica. She had an appointment with a Father James whom she had never met before. This visit could be a turning point in her whole life, depending on the outcome of the interview. Nervous, Patricia prevailed upon her friend, Cecilia McHugh, to accompany her to the monastery.

Visiting a monastery on New Year's Day was not exactly appealing to Cecilia. Although Cecilia was a product of the Catholic school system, she was not overly impressed with some of the Sisters and priests she had met along the way. On that bitter cold day, Cecilia, whom everyone called Ceil, did not share Pat's excitement when they boarded the train from Brooklyn to Jamaica. As they climbed the steep hill up to the Monastery and walked to the front entrance of the austere building, Pat was happy and excited, but Ceil questioned her own sanity for agreeing to make the trip.

As I approached the parlor, I could hear them talking, almost whispering. When I entered the room, the whispering stopped and as products of Catholic schools, they immediately stood. Their formal reception made me smile. I quickly introduced myself, shook their hands and wished them a happy New Year. After Pat introduced herself, I asked her companion's name. When I asked Cecilia if she was also planning to enter the convent, they both laughed and Ceil quickly replied, "No, not me!"

As an icebreaker, I asked them a lot of questions and made small talk to help them relax. I found out they both grew up in Brooklyn, attended Saint Joseph's grade school, and went on to graduate from All Saint's High School. I jokingly asked them if they had to be saints to attend All Saint's. Pat took me seriously and shook her head no; Ceil just let out a hearty laugh. Pat was on her best behavior, but Ceil was definitely not trying to impress me. I had the feeling that Ceil was sizing me up as much as I was trying to evaluate Pat's vocation. After all, it was Pat's visit, so I directed most of my attention to her. Ceil was very alert, listened to our conversation and probably would have a lot of comments to make on her train ride home with Pat.

I then asked Ceil if she would mind sitting alone in the next parlor while I discussed Pat's plan to enter the convent. Ceil was very agreeable and all smiles when I offered her an ash tray.

Pat and I discussed the religious life. I asked Pat the usual questions, like what attracted her to convent life, etc. I made some recommendations to her as to how to prepare for the religious life. I encouraged her to pray for guidance and I advised her to visit me again in a month, if she wished. I asked Pat to give my regards to Sister Geraldine, her sponsor.

I called Ceil back into the parlor and wished them both a safe trip back to Brooklyn. As they disappeared down the hill, I wasn't quite sure if I'd ever see either of them again.

About a week later, Pat called to make a February appointment. On the second visit, Pat and her companion, Ceil, both seemed more relaxed. Pat had decided to enter the convent and informed Sister Geraldine of her decision. After a visit to the Dominican Motherhouse in New Jersey, Pat was accepted as a candidate for the novitiate. I congratulated her and wished her well.

Because of Pat's attraction to the religious life, she wanted to hear about the active, contemplative life of the Passionists. I described the daily schedule in the monastery and the heavy preaching assignments about to start in Lent. I told them both that vocational work would be limited while I was away from Jamaica on preaching assignments. I also expressed my gratitude for the volunteers who would keep the vocational office functioning while I was gone.

Pat was very interested and seemed to have a million questions. Ceil had very little to say. I wasn't sure if she was bored, uninterested, or just content to let her friend take center stage. The visit ended on a happy note. Pat eventually went off to the convent and I never saw her again. Ceil went back to Brooklyn and her office work in the Schlitz Brewery.

Chapter Fifteen

Lent, the peak season for preaching, was over. For the remainder of spring, I would settle down at the vocational desk in Jamaica. There was a mountain of correspondence to be completed and endless phone calls to make. I needed to check references, medical reports, and high school transcripts. No candidates would be considered for Holy Cross or Saint Paul's novitiate unless all the necessary documents were in order. This meant creating a complete file on each of my candidates from the New York metropolitan area, as well as reviewing those funneled to my desk from eight other vocational directors around the northeast.

After the completed paper work was submitted to the seminary and novitiate, there was a period of anxious waiting. It wasn't until the applicants received their welcoming letters of acceptance that both the candidates and their vocational directors relaxed and breathed a sigh of relief. The vocational program proved very successful. The enrollment in the seminary climbed and the drop-out rate declined. The

Passionist vocational directors were hand picked men, who having completed the rigorous training themselves, were well qualified in their selection of those who would follow in their footsteps. A vocational director who is satisfied by the sheer numbers recruited is a "bean counter." He is only concerned with numbers. A vocational director who is a prayerful person recognizes that vocations are God's gifts and that it can take years before he sees the fruit of his labors.

It was some time after her friend, Pat, finalized her plans to enter the convent that Ceil McHugh called to volunteer her services in the vocational office. She said she had done office work since graduating from All Saint's High School. She was volunteering for any type of clerical work that might be required. Unlike the other ladies who lived closer by and volunteered in the evenings, Ceil said she could make the trip on Saturdays if that was agreeable. I told her that I would be grateful for the help. I suggested she come in the following Saturday to size up the situation before making any commitment.

Although I had met Ceil on two previous occasions with her friend Pat, I really had not gotten to know her. She was quiet, sat in the background and let Pat do all the talking. The fact that she kept the appointment on Saturday, her day-off, impressed me. After a tour of the office and an explanation of the volunteer work, I told her there would be many Saturdays when I would be away on assignment. She said my absence would be no problem. As long as there was work to be done and someone available to open the office, she'd be there. She was bright, caught on quickly, and was anxious to get started. I told her to set her own schedule and that if she needed lunch it would be provided. She simply replied, "Don't worry about it."

It took many Saturdays to really get to know Ceil. In casual conversation, before her typing started, I'd ask about her family, her background, and her reasons for volunteering. She said she was one of twelve children. She was the oldest of the seven children living together in a small apartment on Hart Street with her mother. She was the main bread winner of the family and between her and her mother, they were able to provide for her four sisters and two brothers.

Ceil was very honest and didn't try to paint an unreal picture of her life in the crowded apartment on Hart Street. She openly shared many stories about her family with me. I recall one story especially well. Unbeknownst to her mother, one of her sisters was able to conceal the fact that she was playing hooky from school. The truant officer was a nasty man who threatened to take her sister away if Mrs. McHugh didn't correct the situation. Both Ceil and her mother were very upset and were anxious for the truant officer to end his tirade and leave them alone. Ceil then relayed a part of the story that made me smile. She described how she walked the truant officer to the door and watched him maneuver down the snow covered steps. Suddenly, the man slipped and broke his leg! There was a lot of excitement. The ambulance eventually showed up and took him away. He never returned. I asked Ceil if she and her mother laughed afterwards. She replied, "Well, we didn't cry."

Gradually, after many Saturdays, Ceil began to open up more and more. Her mother raised twelve children alone and kept the family together by working as a caretaker or housekeeper of the nurses' residence at Wychoff Hospital. They lived in poverty, stretching welfare checks each month and running a tab at the local grocery. In emergencies, "Big Red," the local cop on the beat, would shake down the neighborhood storekeepers and drop off bread and canned goods to Ceil's family. He was like the Robin Hood of Hart Street – extracting the excesses from the "haves" and without looking for gratitude, delivering them to the doorsteps of the "have nots."

Without realizing it, I was opening the floodgates when I asked Ceil, "Why didn't your mother ask the parish for help?" Her anger, disillusionment and disenchantment with the clergy, the sisters, and the Church came bubbling forth. Her basic faith and charity were intact, but her hope for the future of the Church was shaken.

In her short life, she had experienced too many contradictions between teaching, preaching, and practice. At first, I thought she was just cynical and took her criticism of the Church and clergy personal. I was part of the clerical culture, the closed shop, and I didn't appreciate her evaluation as an outsider. I wasn't entirely successful in submerging my annoyance, but perhaps my efforts to listen did help lighten the burden bearing down on her. It was not until much later, that I realized that I and my fellow Passionists, whom she eventually met, were being put to the test. For too long, she had been let down by the institutional Church and the human element within. As a last resort in her search for peace of mind and heart, she came to the monastery as a volunteer. God works in mysterious ways.

One day, Ceil told me about an elderly woman who lived alone on her block. Ceil occasionally visited the woman when she was in Saint Joseph's grade school. The old woman was poor and did not eat properly. In hope of getting her some food, Ceil led her elderly friend to Saint Joseph's rectory. As they stood on the rectory stoop, waiting for someone to answer the doorbell, they could smell the aroma of a delicious Italian meal being prepared inside. Eventually, a priest stuck his head out of an upstairs window and in broken English asked what they wanted. Ceil yelled back that the old woman was hungry and needed food. He responded, "I don't understand English," and slammed the window shut.

Ceil was hurt and embarrassed for leading the old woman on a wild goose chase. Her heart went out to her old friend who got no closer to food than the whiff of Italian sauce bubbling on the rectory stove. The walk back to the apartment was a sad, quiet one.

I failed in my search for reasons as to why the priest acted in this manner. I could not explain why Saint Joseph's had no programs in place to help the poor and the hungry. Ceil commented that there seemed to be some kind of a high, invisible wall around Saint Joseph's that kept the priests from helping out the poorest parishioners.

Ceil had another shocking experience as an eighth grader. One day, she and her girlfriends were gathered around a piano, singing songs in the parish hall. A parish priest came in and joined the group. As he edged forward and bent over the piano player, in what appeared to be an attempt to read the sheet music, he suddenly slipped his hand under the girl's blouse and fondled her. The girl screamed, spun around, and slapped the priest across the face. He turned red and left the room immediately.

The girl cried hysterically, screaming, "I slapped a priest. I will go to hell!" Ceil and her friends rallied around the girl and told her it was the priest who should worry about going to hell! I told Ceil that there was no excuse for the misbehavior of the priest and that he needed help. She said, "I hope he got it, but my classmate and everyone else who witnessed this needed help, too. But no help ever came."

Even though Saint Joseph's was like a little postage stamp in comparison to the world wide Catholic Church, it was the only spiritual center in Ceil's neighborhood. It was the only place for baptisms, first communions, May processions, weddings, and funerals. Ceil always saw the little old Italian ladies, dressed in black, as the real spiritual backbone of the parish. They started their day with morning Mass and could be seen almost anytime during the day hunched over in prayer. The parish was a tight little community and Saint Joseph's alone represented the Catholic Church, for better or for worse. Ceil wasn't totally negative about her parish. Sometimes, I think she enjoyed just rattling my cage. If she got too critical, I would call her "Sister Negativity." She would usually respond with a hearty laugh and go back to typing.

Ceil never read about Liberation Theology or heard talk about preferential option for the poor. She knew nothing of Dorothy Day and her "Houses of Hospitality." She had not heard phrases such as, "We need to live simply so that others may simply live." But, in her own insightful way, Ceil recognized the living of the Gospels in the lives of others. She was deeply impressed by the devoted care the "Little Sisters of the Poor" gave to their elderly residents.

However, Ceil had little patience for the preachers of the gospel who didn't practice what they preached. She thought the beautiful vestments of the clergy and the spotlessly clean habits of the religious were a sham unless the people inside them were serious about living the Gospel. She always spoke very kindly of an elderly Passionist who never passed the vocational office without waving and offering to bring her a refreshment. She said this priest, Father Lambert, seemed very happy in his vocation and seemed able to blend holiness, kindness, and friendliness in a refreshing way. Her assessment of him was right on target.

Almost without exception, Ceil would arrive early Saturday morning and stay until approximately four in the afternoon. I didn't know where she found all the energy, especially following a full week doing office work in Schlitz Brewery. In the event that I couldn't be present, she would do all the clerical work, answer the phone, send out vocational packets, etc. – all without the need for supervision.

On one Saturday, I returned to the office to find Ceil still working. It was pouring outside and I told her she would be drenched before she even reached the train station. I offered to drive her home. She declined but when I insisted she became quite agreeable. I told her to meet me in the front of the monastery. As I pulled up, she automatically opened the front door to get in. I asked her to sit in the back seat to avoid any scandal. I couldn't interpret the look on her face – surprise, confusion, insult or annoyance. But then, she responded, in her own frank way, "How stupid." The mere possibility of someone negatively twisting my offer upset her. I simply said, "You know how people talk, how they can get the wrong impression." She angrily responded, "That never crossed my mind. Who are these people? Are they the same people who practically fall down worshipping you guys one minute and the next accuse you of evil where there is none? Trouble is, they judge others by their own actions."

The remainder of the ride was very quiet. I kept wondering if I was part of that group which is too quick to pass judgment and too slow to give others the benefit of the doubt.

When we got to Hart Street, the door to the apartment on the first floor led directly into the kitchen. Sitting there was Ceil's mother, a lovely little Irish lady who brought twelve children into the world. She was sitting at the kitchen table with three or four of her children. My sudden appearance in the doorway was a total surprise. They had no phone, so Ceil could not give them any advance warning. All conversation stopped and all eyes widened when they saw the Roman collar. In those days, when a priest suddenly appeared at the door, it was usually to bring bad news or officiate at a wake.

Ceil quickly said, "This is Father James." Her mother was all smiles, nudged one of her daughters to get up, and had me sit at the table next to her. Ceil made a few wisecracks, hoping to help everyone relax. I told them about my work and the great help that Ceil was. Within a few minutes, there was standing room only – brothers and sisters kept appearing from other rooms. Ceil's brother, Harry, was a comedian and lit up the whole room. Pretty soon a fresh pot of coffee was perking on the stove. At a nod from the mother, one of the kids disappeared out the door and reappeared shortly with a pound cake from the grocery. I enjoyed the coffee and the cake, but most of all, I enjoyed the company.

I must admit that Ceil's mother stole my attention. I marveled at this little lady who was able, almost single handedly, to raise and keep together such a large family. She knew poverty and all the hardships that go with it, but the smiles and joy she radiated as each of her children spoke, told me where her strength came from. She loved her children and they loved her. That was all that mattered.

It was a great visit and a real eye opener. It helped me to understand Ceil, where she was coming from, and from whom she had inherited her strength, generosity, and sense of humor. The visit also taught me that many of the walls that separate the Church from the poor could be broken down if more priests would find time to share a cup of coffee in the kitchen of some parishioners.

A week after the visit, I said to Ceil, "I hope my impromptu visit to your home didn't upset your family." She answered, "Don't worry about it. If they didn't like you, they would have slipped out of the kitchen. You didn't see anyone leave, did you?"

It became more and more apparent to me that I had a long way to go before I could even come close to walking in the footsteps of the Good Shepherd who was always in search of the lost sheep. It was easy for me to become complacent in my relationship with God in the insulated atmosphere of the monastery. But just outside the front door of the monastery, were the streets where Jesus would have mingled with the poor and the neglected – the wandering sheep. More and more, I realized that my love for God and my love for my neighbor must be intertwined.

Chapter Sixteen

It was in my tenth year as a priest, that I began to evaluate my ministry. It was ten years of an active, rewarding, and hopefully, productive ministry. I was fully engaged in the primary apostolate of the Passionists – preaching missions and retreats, plus doing vocational work. This was the type of ministry that Passionist seminarians aim for, but never in my wildest dreams, did I anticipate such an active apostolate.

Most of my energy was directed towards students who had spent most of their lives in a Catholic school environment. These students had daily contact with priests and the message of the gospel. Because attendance at Catholic school retreats was compulsory, there was always a certain percentage of retreatants who were resistant. Conducting an adult retreat was like shepherding a mild mannered flock of sheep, whereas a youth retreat was like taming a herd of wild horses.

I recall one old, cranky retreat director who always disappeared into his room during youth retreats conducted on his premises. He opened the retreat house to youth groups only under orders and after much protest. During one such youth retreat, he came storming out of his room and screamed down the full length of the corridor at me for chatting with a group of students. I wasn't sure if his anger stemmed from our talking in the hallway or if it was due to our disturbing his sleep. The young men were startled and wide eyed when he yelled at me, "I'm reporting you to the Passionist General in Rome for the way you run retreats."

He went back into his room and slammed his door so hard, it was a wonder it didn't come off its hinges. I shrugged my shoulders in disbelief and continued my discussion with the teens elsewhere. If any of these young men were thinking of joining the Passionists, I'm sure this outburst stopped them in their tracks.

I never did receive a reprimand from the Passionist General. Maybe the cantankerous retreat director had second thoughts about his threatening behavior.

In the early sixties, I became increasingly concerned about the young Catholics who were slowly drifting away from the Church. These were turbulent times, especially for the young. They were confused and challenged by the rapidly changing moral standards confronting them. They were desperately in need of guidance.

The majority of teens in most parishes attended public schools. It was only natural for them to gravitate to their own school. This was where their friends were, this was where they socialized, and this was where they participated in after school programs and sporting events. There was little time remaining for parish programs. In spite of the heroic efforts of parents and some clergy, teen participation in parish life was on the decline.

I wasn't foolish enough to think I could turn the tide and fill the church with the young. But I kept thinking, if only I could find a place to dedicate to the teens most at risk. It had to be a place where they could have a sustained, intense religious experience. It couldn't be a typical adult retreat house. I knew that would be a turn-off. Everything about the place had to be geared towards the young and it needed to be operated by a select staff that could relate to them. It would have to be a place that would attract the very young parishioners that we worried most about.

The more I thought about starting a retreat house for the most vulnerable youth in the church, the more the prospect appealed to me. I quietly conducted a feasibility study, checking with others involved in youth work. I spoke with public school teachers, coaches, youth ministers, cops, and priests. I was anxious to start an apostolate that would serve the Church's youth. I felt it was especially necessary to reach out to the youth in public high schools and secular colleges – the segment of the population that receives the most criticism and the least help. The adults who ran successful youth programs were enthusiastic and said the project would be an answer to many prayers. Adults who wrote off teen programs as lost causes weren't very encouraging and had many reservations about running such a program. I got the most enthusiastic support from the teens in the poorest parishes, located in the roughest neighborhoods. After explaining the retreat program, it became apparent that these young apostolic roughnecks were interested in making youth retreats a reality.

The next step was to locate a site for a youth retreat center. After scouring the Brooklyn Diocese for vacant buildings or under-utilized property, I found nothing. Next, I turned my attention to the newly formed Diocese of Rockville Center, which spanned across Nassau and Suffolk counties of Long Island. Without looking any further, I thought of thirty-two beautiful, waterfront acres located on Shelter Island. Shelter Island was a quaint little island, just a short ferry ride from the eastern most tip of Long Island.

The property was owned by the Passionists and used only two months out of the year, as a summer vacation spot. There was a new, free standing kitchen and a dining hall capable of serving at least a hundred people. This building was the only building on the thirty-two acres that was "winterized." Located on a knoll, a short distance away, was a beautiful, rustic chapel. And completing the triangle, was a simple, wood frame building containing twenty-five small rooms and a lounge. The potential for developing a teen retreat center was definitely there.

Unlike adults, who are influenced by comfortable accommodations and interior furnishings, teens, especially those from congested city streets, would be completely captivated by the wide open spaces and the big sky that comes with the seashore. When I would describe the area, teens were ready to pack their bags and go to Shelter Island. Adults were cautious in their views, sometimes getting sidetracked by what seemed like insurmountable obstacles.

The most common objection against opening a retreat center on remote Shelter Island was the ninety mile trip from the city to the retreat house. I found myself being swayed by this argument until I recalled that when I was a teen, a four hundred mile trip to the seminary was more of an adventure than a problem. I realized that if this retreat project was ever going to get off the ground, I better climb inside the minds of teens and envision this apostolate through their eyes. Excitement was beginning to mount.

My longtime classmate and friend, Father Stan, was the administrator of the Passionist property on Shelter Island. He was very familiar with the buildings and their maintenance and had an excellent relationship with the local tradesmen. He was delighted with my plan to winterize the buildings for a year round retreat center. After consulting with local carpenters, plumbers, and electricians, he assured me that the under utilized buildings could be transformed into a youth retreat center. One more hurdle was overcome.

After hashing and rehashing all the pros and cons for establishing the youth retreat center on Shelter Island, I put a written proposal in the hands of my superior in Jamaica. He passed it on to the Provincial and his consultants.

During the early sixties, young Americans, who were the fastest growing segment of the population, were being pulled in all different directions. Young people were becoming more independent and assertive, even rebellious. Parents, educators, and clergy had good reason to worry about the future of our youth. All agreed our youth needed help. Any priest in touch with reality, had to admit that there was a steady decline in the number of teens in attendance at Sunday Mass. A youth apostolate on Shelter Island was needed.

A youth retreat center dedicated primarily to young men attending public school, while unique to the entire country, would be in harmony with the Passionist ministry of conducting retreats. The sustained spiritual contact with youths on retreat would not only become a source of vocations, but would also become a stepping stone for men's retreats in the future.

The cost of winterizing two buildings and adapting them for retreatants was minimal, considering both the spiritual good flowing from the retreats, as well as the utilization of property that had remained idle for ten months out of every year!

Finally, I requested that the Retreat be named in honor of Saint Gabriel, the Patron of Youth. Saint Gabriel was a Passionist seminarian who died while preparing for the priesthood. In a relatively short time, my proposal was approved and I was told to start preparations for the opening of Saint Gabriel's Retreat for Young Men. I was advised to make a courtesy call on Bishop Kellenberg of Rockville Centre in order to inform him of our intention to open Saint Gabriel's on Shelter Island in 1963. The superior of the Jamaica monastery joined me on my visit to the bishop. I remember this meeting as though it was yesterday.

When we were ushered in to meet Bishop Kellenberg in his temporary chancery office, he was seated behind a large desk. He looked stern, seemed preoccupied, and not quite sure what the reason for our visit was. My immediate impression was not encouraging.

After introducing ourselves, I started to explain that we were asking for his blessing on the youth retreat house we were planning to open on Shelter Island. I explained that this apostolate was designed to help young men attending public high schools and secular colleges. I stressed the need to reach out to these young men, that they were the hope for our future and that they needed an intense, sustained, religious experience.

I was shocked and my chin must have hit my chest, when the bishop slammed his two hands down on his desk and loudly said, "Don't tell me about the youth of the diocese. I know their needs. I'm just in the process of establishing a new diocese and everyone is looking for a piece of this pie. This is not the time." He sounded like his mind was made up and the visit was over.

I wasn't about to cave in and reminded him that the Passionists owned the property for half a century and that the necessary buildings already existed. I assured him that our plans would, in no way, interfere with his plan to develop the Rockville Centre Diocese. He started to look as though he might be reconsidering.

Next, I tried to tug on his heart strings. I told him that I had recently preached a novena at Saint Philip Neri in the Bronx. I asked the congregation to pray for a special intention of mine – the opening of Saint Gabriel's. At the conclusion of the novena, an elderly lady who faithfully attended each night, introduced herself as the mother of Bishop Kellenberg! She told me that she would continue to pray for my intention. The Bishop finally smiled, stood up, and shook my hand. He said, "If my mother is praying for it, how can I be against it? Go ahead with Saint Gabriel's."

He gave us his blessing and I felt like I was walking on air as we departed. I wonder if the Bishop ever told his mother that her prayers had been answered!

Chapter Seventeen

On April 28, 1963, the Provincial gave his official approval for the establishment of Saint Gabriel's on Shelter Island. There was a great deal of excitement among my fellow Passionists. They all seemed to be in favor of this new and long overdue apostolate for youth. The promises of help and offers of prayers from so many, even the Provincial, were not only encouraging but gave me a great sense of community.

Things were falling into place very quickly on both sides of the Hudson River. Over in Union City, New Jersey, the Provincial and his consultants were busy looking for a priest to replace me in Jamaica as the Vocational Director. They also extended Father Stan's summer assignment on Shelter Island to a year round appointment. Eventually, a Passionist Brother and another priest would be added to the staff.

Life was hectic in Jamaica, as well. I was officially assigned as Retreat Director of Saint Gabriel's and told to report to Shelter Island on May 1st. In the short time remaining, my faithful volunteer, Ceil, made sure there was a smooth transition in the vocational office. I had no qualms of conscience about leaving the vocational work, knowing that my volunteers were there to assist my replacement. I always knew I wasn't indispensable and the way my replacement adjusted so quickly, definitely reinforced that opinion. However, during my eight years in Jamaica, I had made many fine friends. Saying goodbye was not easy.

Leaving Jamaica, driving ninety miles, and taking a ferry across a strip of water to Shelter Island was like traveling to a whole new world. The gray sky of New York City was replaced with a bright blue and unpolluted sky. The constant whine of the jets out of Kennedy and LaGuardia Airports soon gave way to nothing more than the occasional cry of a sea gull, circling above. Man made noises were reduced to a minimum, leaving room for the sounds of nature. I began to understand the fascination visitors had for an island named "Shelter."

The prospect of starting any kind of a youth center on Shelter Island did not generate an enthusiastic response from the local residents. Their notion of a youth retreat, varied from visions of Father Flanagan's "Boys Town," to a rehab center for juvenile delinquents. My appearance on the Island in my black suit and Roman collar gave credence to the rumor that an out of town cleric was serious about starting some kind of youth program. For the first few weeks, it took a lot of smiles, handshakes, and small talk to break down the silent treatment and melt the icy stares. Thank God, Father Stan, whom the local residents knew and trusted, was able to assure them that Saint Gabriel's would in no way threaten their peaceful lifestyle.

When local carpenters, plumbers, and electricians were hired to winterize the retreat house, the residents all started to relax. Word spread quickly that the Passionist priests were not afraid to get their hands dirty. The local contractors were impressed when they saw "Stan the man" appear in his work clothes, get down on his knees, and expertly lay the floor tiles. It was difficult for anyone to stand around with his hands in his pockets and watch Stan tackle one project after another. He never had to ask for help. His eagerness to complete the renovations was contagious. Men of all faiths, mostly retirees, began to appear out of nowhere to volunteer their services. Men like Harry Smithwick, Al Murphy, Ed Gross, and Tony Labrozzi, to name a few, worked well with Father Stan and our caretaker Rocco Satira. Saint Gabriel's was beginning to take shape.

While I, too, enjoyed pitching in with Stan and his volunteers, my immediate focus was to inform the public of the birth and existence of our unique youth apostolate. This meant preparing descriptive brochures and enclosing them in letters to parish priests, youth ministers and chaplains. Editors of diocesan newspapers throughout the metropolitan area were very cooperative in accepting articles featuring Saint Gabe's. I put together a slide show featuring the beautiful Shelter Island and the setting for the retreats. For most audiences, the concept of a religious retreat was vague and unappealing. But once we showed them pictures of the thirty-two beautiful acres on the sea shore, the young audience would come alive. Hardly a week went by that I didn't load up my car with the slide projector and brochures and try to sell the message of the little retreat house on Shelter Island. I would speak to any group that would listen.

In the mid 1960s, adults were worried about the corruption of young people all across America. Parents, clergy, education, and law enforcement were concerned about the drug use, the juvenile delinquency, the street violence, and the campus unrest. "Youth" was the magic word and anyone attempting to help young people received a lot of encouragement from concerned adults.

Father Lucian, who spent most of his priesthood in retreat work, prevailed upon the men of the Molloy Retreat House in Jamaica to donate ten thousand dollars to help launch the youth retreats on Shelter Island. An elderly shut-in whom I visited regularly, while stationed in Jamaica years before, passed away. She remembered Saint Gabriel's in her will and wanted her gift of five thousand dollars to be used to sponsor retreats for impoverished young men. Just before the assassination of President Kennedy, we received a letter from the White

House encouraging our mission. During this same period, the Agent in charge of the F.B.I.'s New York office invited me into Manhattan. He liked what he heard about our youth retreats and supported our program in a number of ways.

Too many unexplained gifts and blessings were showered on Saint Gabriel's for anyone to question, even for a moment, that this was God's work. There was no way to rationalize the sudden, almost explosive, ways in which the men and women of Shelter Island rallied to support the retreat program. The editor of the New York Sunday News featured a two page picture story that brought Saint Gabriel's to the breakfast tables of thousands. The Krpata family, the owners of a bus company, offered to transport the retreatants to Shelter Island on a non-profit basis. I never ceased to be amazed at the cross section of adults that so generously and spontaneously surfaced to help our youth mission.

But most encouraging of all, was the enthusiastic response that came from the young men for whom Saint Gabriel's was formed. These were the young men who lived on the outer fringe of parish life, the faceless young men who lived on the streets surrounding the church they rarely entered. At last, they were singled out to visit a place they could call their own – a little island where they could talk freely about their problems, share their plans, and renew their friendship with a God they thought they were losing. These were the "sleeping giants" the

Church worried about. Their potential for radiating goodness was immeasurable. These tough, streetwise kids became the best boosters Saint Gabriel's ever had. In their own unique and surprising way, these apostolic roughnecks were sharing the Gospel message with their parents, teachers, coaches, friends, and even the clergy.

During the sixties, most seniors attending Catholic High School were expected to make a private retreat before graduating. News of a youth retreat house spread like wildfire throughout the Catholic school system. Administrators of Catholic High Schools began calling to reserve dates to accommodate their seniors. For a retreat house just beginning and struggling to make ends meet, this avalanche of requests was an answer to many prayers. It would mean no more recruiting, no more running around. It would mean a guaranteed full house, a steady income – the course of least resistance. The temptation was there.

Holding the line for the public school students was not easy, but I was determined. Reserving all weekends for the Catholic school seniors, would be like letting the "proverbial camel" get its nose under the tent. Once the camel got in, the public school students would, once again, be on the outside looking in. To avoid this, we allowed Catholic school seniors who were excused from class to make retreats, to attend mid-week retreats. They readily did so. As for young women, there were a number of Women Retreat Houses run by the Sisters throughout the metropolitan area. I had no intention of competing with the Sisters for female retreatants, nor did I think Saint Gabriel's was suitable for co-ed retreats.

I can still see the bus that rolled onto the property for the first retreat. I was very excited until the bus stopped and only eleven young men stepped out. At first, I was discouraged. However, for the remainder of the weekend, I kept reminding these courageous pioneers that Jesus began his worldwide ministry with only eleven apostles. These eleven were reluctantly convinced by an adult to make a retreat. Now, it would be their turn to become teenage apostles, ready to share their retreat experience with others. This first group gave birth to the "Apostolic Session," which became the final session of all retreats to follow. Saint Gabriel's would have failed in its mission if its purpose was to bring teens out to Shelter Island to gobble up all kinds of spiritual goodies and not share their new found peace and joy with their peers. If this was what God had wanted for the first apostles, Christianity would never have gotten outside the walls of Jerusalem!

At the conclusion of the first retreat, one teen said, "I really didn't want to come here, but now I don't want to leave." I responded, "Glad you got something good out of it. But don't come back unless you bring a friend." He got the message.

One day I got a phone call from a principal of a vocational high school in Manhattan. He said, "I just read about Saint Gabriel's in the Sunday news. I have twenty students in my school who want to make a retreat. Will you take them?" I happily answered, "Sure, I'll book them for a weekend," and I gave him a date. He answered, "There is only one problem – None of these kids can afford the $20 stipend." After doing some quick math, I took a deep breath, knowing Saint Gabriel's would be down four hundred dollars. But still, I said, "Send the kids and you're welcome to join them." His group turned out to be one of the best, apostolic groups of young men ever to come to Saint Gabriel's.

On Monday, the day after the retreat with the vocational students, I opened the morning mail and found a five hundred dollar donation to Saint Gabriel's from an anonymous donor. It was another reminder of God's mysterious workings. Saint Gabriel's was not designed to be a money maker, nor was a teen ever turned away for a lack of it. Regardless, somehow our funds continued to grow. Why wouldn't they? God's work was being done.

Chapter Eighteen

"That same day, on leaving the house, Jesus sat down by the lakeshore. Such great crowds gathered around him that he went and took a seat in a boat while the crowd stood on the shore. He addressed them at length in parables, speaking in this fashion ... the reign of God is like a mustard seed which someone took and sowed in his field. It is the smallest seed of all, yet when full-grown; it is the largest of all plants. It becomes so big a shrub that the birds of the sky come and build their nests in its branches." (Mathew 13:1-32).

Saint Gabriel's was like the mustard seed; it was the smallest retreat house of all. And yet when full grown, it became a haven which attracted the young and the old, the saints and the sinners, from near and far. Teens from the entire metropolitan area packed the retreat house six days out of every week. Men and women from Shelter Island and the east end of Long Island booked the monthly evenings of recollection. And one Sunday afternoon each month, the Sisters from an assortment of religious communities in eastern Suffolk County, flocked to Shelter Island for a mini-retreat. The most notable member of the clergy to make private retreats to Saint Gabriel's was John McGann, the future bishop of the Rockville Centre Diocese.

In 1964, one year after Saint Gabriel's opened its doors, I was invited to Detroit to introduce our youth apostolate to the National Conference of Catholic retreatants. Adult retreatants from all over the country were totally captivated by Saint Gabriel's mission for public school teens. The possibility of teen retreatants becoming future adult retreatants was obvious to all. The little retreat house on Shelter Island received nationwide publicity. I was selected to be the National Moderator of youth retreats and was expected to meet periodically throughout the year with Bishop John Wright, the moderator of adult retreatants. The mustard seed of Shelter Island not only took root, but with God's help, was spreading its branches near and far.

The late 60's continued to be turbulent times. There were campus riots. Young men were leaving for and dying in Vietnam, while others dashed across the Canadian border. S.D.S., Students for a Democratic Society, was stirring things up on the west coast. It was intense. But in spite of all the confusion and turmoil, there were still great stories in the men coming to Shelter Island. It took courage for young men to step away from their home town crowd and go to a retreat. Some came to make their peace with God before leaving for Vietnam. Others were led to Saint Gabriel's by someone else's example. For example, there was a young New York City policeman who led a group of teens from Bayridge, Brooklyn to Shelter Island. This young cop eventually turned in his badge for a Roman collar and became a priest. One of the teens in his group also eventually became a priest and a major religious superior in the Passionist congregation. During this period, an American flag was hanging in the dining hall for all the young retreatants to see. It was the flag that covered the casket of a young, Shelter Island marine who was killed in Vietnam. His parents, who actively supported Saint Gabriel's, wanted his flag to be associated with all the young men seeking God on Shelter Island. There were many, many stories that could be told by the thousands of people visiting Saint Gabriel's each year.

The young men who came to Shelter Island in the 1960's were not mystics who could contemplate a God they could not see, nor relate to a divine person they could not imagine. They lived in a sensate culture which catered to hairstyles, clothing, cars, and all the other things that made the shopping malls so attractive.

However, their active imaginations could relate to a Jesus who demonstrated their human nature. They could relate to a young man who worked in a carpenter's shop in Nazareth. They could appreciate his kindness in changing water into wine at the wedding of the poor young couple in Cana of Galilee. They could empathize with the fright of Peter in his denial of

Christ. They could admire the courage of Simon who stepped out of the bystanders to help Jesus bear the Cross. These young retreatants, with their strong, healthy bodies, would even shudder with the thought of the pain that accompanied the scourging of Jesus, the crown of thorns, and the nailing of His hands and feet to a wooden beam. And having come to Shelter Island, weighed down with remorse over past misdeeds, these young men could experience the peace and sheer joy that overcame the repentant thief on Calvary when Jesus turned to him and said all is forgiven. *"This day you will be with me in paradise."*

The power of these experiences led Father Stan, Rocco the caretaker, the teens, and I, to cut the Stations of the Cross out of the hillside overlooking the property. It also led a kind benefactor to donate a life sized image of a youthful Jesus nailed to the cross. We placed it at the highest point of the property.

Whenever a teen felt abandoned, guilt ridden, or misunderstood by a distant God, I would challenge him to walk up the hillside quietly and alone in order to think about how Pontius Pilate condemned Jesus to death because of peer pressure. I told them to think about Simon, who had the courage to step out of the crowd to help Jesus carry the Cross. I encouraged them to pause and think about Jesus' suffering when the nails were pounded into His hands and feet. Finally,

I challenged them to stare at the figure on the Cross and yet continue to contend that, "God doesn't love me."

In less than two years, Saint Gabriel's was busting at the seams. It could no longer accommodate all the teens who wanted to make a retreat. I got the Provincial's permission to double the size of the retreat house, providing a total of fifty single rooms. When the Provincial promised to double the amount of any funds I raised myself, I knew I could raise the money necessary for the expansion. The first thing I did was to go out and buy a brand new Ford Mustang. It was a bright red, flashy car with white interior – a real eye catcher.

Every Sunday, I arranged to speak at all the Masses at different parishes. I told the parishioners the story of Saint Gabriel's and asked them to buy "chances" for the beautiful Mustang parked outside the Church. Teenage retreatants, clothed in Saint Gabriel jackets, were stationed at all exits to sell chances. Few could resist the enthusiastic teens at the doors. The cooperative pastors were overwhelmed by the response of their parishioners.

During the week, my volunteers and friends from Jamaica came to the rescue. Ceil McHugh and her co-workers had the Mustang parked outside Schlitz Brewery on payday. A ton of brewery workers bought chances. Another friend from Jamaica arranged to have the flashy Mustang parked outside the main exit of Pfizer Pharmaceuticals on Flushing Avenue.

Saint Gabriel's had a lot of friends in Brooklyn. The Mustang also got a lot of weekday exposure when parked in front of the Jamaica Monastery. Both parishioners and retreatants were very generous. After a raffle at the end of an exhausting summer, we were given the green light to start the expansion of Saint Gabriel's.

There's a saying: "Run a fundraiser and you'll find out who your friends are." I say, "Show people how you are helping kids, and you'll never be able to count all the strangers who extend helping hands."

One day after a retreat, I was in my office, tired and daydreaming. As I stared out my window, there was a knock on the door and a gentleman asked if he could speak with me. He said he attended Mass in our little Chapel and was very impressed with our teen missions. He explained that he was blessed in many ways and would like to share his blessings with those less fortunate. He lived in the Mashomack Preserve on Shelter Island, a piece of property approximately three thousand acres large. Besides the main residence where he lived, he had a second residence capable of accommodating twelve visitors on weekends. He asked for suggestions on how he might use this second home. I told him that Saint Gabriel's opened its doors to teens for retreats and to adults, both lay and religious, for periods of recollection. But there was one segment of the population untouched by Saint Gabriel's – little children. I described the poorest of the poor young children, mostly Hispanic, who attended the public schools in Brooklyn. They lived in ghettos, an asphalt jungle with only a crowded school yard for a playground.

I mentioned the story in the Gospel of Mark, where Jesus became annoyed with the apostles when they attempted to keep children away from him. He said, "Let the children come to see me and do not hinder them....whoever welcomes a child such as this for my sake welcomes me." Mr. Daly smiled, nodded his head in agreement, and said he would welcome the children. Once I saw the beautiful accommodations being offered, I assured him that Saint Gabriel's would be honored to assist him in his apostolate to the children. I offered to do all the leg work and make all the arrangements to get his program started.

On her weekly visits to the vocational office in Jamaica, Ceil McHugh often described the poor children she could see from her office in the Schlitz Brewery, which bordered on the school playground. Judging from her description, these children would be perfect candidates for a weekend visit to Mashomack Preserve – the open spaces, beautiful accommodations, and nutritious meals would do them a world of good. I called Ceil and asked her if she, with the help of another adult volunteer, would be willing to escort and chaperone twelve children on weekend visits to Shelter Island. I told her she would be in charge of an independent operation, entirely separate from Saint Gabriel's. As expected, she jumped at the opportunity to help poor children. In a very short time, she recruited her co-workers at Schlitz to assist her as volunteers. Because my involvement in running the teen retreats took up almost all of my time, I knew the success of the children's program would rest entirely on Ceil's shoulders. I had no doubt that she could effectively run the program.

After securing the full cooperation of the public school principal and the parents' permission, the neediest and most deserving pupils were selected. Special arrangements were then made with the Long Island Railroad for transportation from Brooklyn to Greenport Ferry. Within two months, the children were on their way to Mashomack Preserve.

The entire weekend was filled with new and exciting experiences for the children. It started with the long train ride from their crowded little world to the open spaces of Suffolk County. This was followed by an exciting Ferry boat ride from Greenport to Shelter Island. The little travelers were quickly put at ease by the warm welcome they received as they entered the weekend home. After finishing their first meal, the children were given a guided tour through the preserve. For the first time, they saw prancing deer. To the delight of the children, they saw their first real live, "Bambis!"

Father Adrian, a member of Saint Gabriel's retreat team, was deeply impressed by the little visitors to Mashomack Preserve. The gentle ease that this young priest displayed with the poor city children later blossomed into his full time ministry with the poor of Appalachia.

The poor of all ages are quick to sense when they have a special place in the hearts of those who minister to them. Impoverished people, young or old, do not feel cheated or short changed or patronized in the presence of a truly detached millionaire. Nor are they made to feel inferior or put down by the tireless energy of the volunteer who works in their behalf. And feelings of abandonment by God begin to fade when a Christ-like member of the clergy reaches out to them.

Ceil tells one very memorable story from a Mashomack retreat. On a Sunday afternoon, at the conclusion of their visit, the last child to leave the weekend home, closed the front door, gently patted it, kissed it, and said, "Goodbye beautiful house. I love you!" That says it all.

Chapter Nineteen

It was the end of 1967. The week between Christmas and New Year's was a quiet time for Saint Gabriel's. No retreats, nor any other activities, were booked for the week. It was the week the entire retreat team got a well-deserved rest.

I told the entire staff, priests and brothers, to plan their Christmas vacations - to relax, get off the Island, and enjoy a relaxing visit with their families. I assured them that Saint Gabriel's would still be there when they returned and that I would "mind the fort." I didn't have to twist any arms. Bags were packed, transportation plans completed, and by Christmas Eve, I saw the last of them off.

I'll never forget the peaceful silence of that Christmas morning. There were absolutely no distractions. On the way to visit our little chapel on the hill, it was easy to sense the presence of God. If there is such a thing as a silent conversation, it took place for me that morning. Quietly, in a silence that was almost audible, I was able to share my thoughts, my doubts, and my inner struggles. I held nothing back and asked my God to guide me. The interior conflicts, the doubts, the questions about my future which had plagued me for a long time, seemed to evaporate. A deep sense of peace and relief came over me. God was a good listener!

As I walked out of the chapel into the cold, crisp air, it was so quiet that I could easily hear the crunching of the snow beneath each foot step. Free from the endless activity that goes along with a teen retreat, I was able to stand at the water's edge and actually hear the crackling of the ice, which always accompanied the change of tides in Coecles Harbor. From the clear, blue sky overhead, right down to the pure white snow, it seemed as though the Creator could not have provided me with a better setting for what became a turning point in my life. Lingering doubts disappeared. Blurry thoughts gave way to clear decisions. A life change, which was underway, would remain as a secret between God and me for some time. I would need many more conversations with my God and quiet time at the Harbor's edge, before sharing my plans with others.

It was almost noon when I entered the administration building. I was alone. The dining hall was quiet - no teenagers, no staff, no friends. The kitchen was lifeless - no brothers preparing meals, no delivery trucks at the back door. The phone was silent. I was completely alone on Christmas.

I picked up the phone and called my brother's home where my entire family was gathered. When my brother Bud answered,

I could hear the excitement of my nephews and nieces, the laughter and merry conversations of the adults. Everything got quiet when Bud shouted, "Father Jim's on the phone."

After wishing Mom and Pop a Merry Christmas and a blessed New Year, we made the typical small talk. Mom ended the conversation with her usual last question, "How are you?" I answered, "Couldn't be better." But as I hung up, the loneliness filled me.

I no sooner started to make a sandwich for lunch, when the phone rang for the very first time that Christmas day. It was Ceil McHugh. She said, "Just called to wish you a Merry Christmas and Happy New Year." Ceil's initiative in making this call made me very happy. She was the only person to reach out to me that day. I extended my greetings to her, her mother and family.

While eating my sandwich alongside the kitchen window, I noticed a police cruiser slowly entering the property. I went outside to greet Bob Brown, the chief of the Shelter Island Police. When he found out I was alone, he immediately invited me to join him and his family for Christmas dinner. Because I had to "mind the fort," I politely declined his request. But his invitation, along with Ceil's call, were the two bright spots of that beautiful Christmas day.

Shelter Island is a very quiet place, especially during the winter. Living alone on thirty-two acres for that week between

Christmas and New Year's was pure solitude. There was plenty of time for reflection. Twenty years had passed since I made my profession as a Passionist. When I took those vows, I had no reservation, no doubts about it being a lifetime commitment. When I was ordained a priest, fifteen years earlier, I knew that the priesthood would be a part of me until the day I died. God was with me in the past, was sustaining me in the present, and I certainly trusted that God would be at my side in the future.

Like the repentant thief, crucified alongside Jesus on Calvary, who was very aware of his own limitations but never put limits on God's love, I too felt very comfortable and reassured in placing my future in God's hands.

Going into the New Year, I knew 1968 would be a turning point in my life. The nagging persistent thoughts and doubts that had burdened me for more than a year were gone. My plans for the future were quickly coming together. There was no way I could continue to give Saint Gabriel's one hundred percent of my undistracted time and energy. But to give anything less than one hundred percent to Saint Gabriel's and its entire people was unacceptable to me. Following a lot of quiet time in the chapel, my mind was made up - I would request a leave of absence.

In the minds of many priests and religious in 1968, requesting a leave of absence was interpreted as the first step in a process which would culminate in a complete departure from the religious life and priesthood. For some, seeking a leave of absence was nothing more than what is known today as a Sabbatical. Before formally requesting a leave of absence from the Provincial, I wanted my parents and brothers to be the first to hear of my plans. Not knowing how my family, especially my mother, would react to my decision, I wanted to be the one to inform them rather than risk having them hear it from someone else.

Just before speaking to my parents, a Provincial consulter phoned me from Union City. He was very happy and congratulated me for being elected as a delegate to the upcoming Provincial Chapter. He said that I had received a large number of votes and that this was an indication of the high regard that my fellow religious had for me. I thanked him for the information and secretly hoped that my Passionist brothers would not be upset when they learned of my plans to seek leave. To freely share my plans and observations with my fellow religious could be unsettling for some and even scandalous to others. I chose to remain quiet.

I admired my fellow priests and religious who appeared very happy and didn't experience any doubts about their future. On the other hand, scattered reports were coming in about some friends of mine who were also seeking six-month leaves. They were good, holy priests who served the Church well. Apparently, they too felt the need for a time-out, a change of pace, and an extended retreat from the active ministry. Some returned from their leave, spiritually refreshed and eager to dive right back into an active apostolate. Others, ended their search for peace of mind and soul by becoming monks in the quiet solitude of monastic life. And still others, never returned.

Seeking a leave of absence was a new phenomenon in the early sixties and quickly gained momentum in the years to come. In the early 60s, the walls of rectories, monasteries, and convents were bulging with vocations. Candidates for seminaries and novitiates were falling over one another in order to gain entry. There was no shortage of priests or religious. Thus, the fact that a little trickle began to seek leave, while often creating anger and shock, didn't create any real soul searching on the part of the Church. Those in positions of authority didn't ask, "Why? Why is this happening?" There was too much complacency. The few leaving were expendable. No one had an inkling of the mass exodus that was to follow. In less than twenty years, the complacency was replaced by a frantic search for candidates to fill the empty halls of the seminaries and novitiates. Standards were lowered and the search for candidates became desperate.

There were no easy answers or reasons for the decisions to seek leave. Those leaving were as much a mixed group as those staying. There was no special age group, temperament, or form of ministry that could be associated with the growing exodus. For most, the decision to leave was not a rash or impulsive one.

It was the culmination of a lot of soul searching and internal anguish that accompanied the decision to alter one's lifestyle.

A lot of discussion ensued among the clergy and religious, especially depending upon the reputation of the one leaving. There were the Monday morning quarterbacks who had all the answers, "I could see it coming, it was obvious, the writing was on the wall, and it was just a matter of time." Pointing the finger of blame or making snap, rash judgments after the fact was much easier than extending a helping hand at the time of need.

There were also the superficial critics who covered up their own inadequacies with frivolous remarks like, "Their reasons for leaving were not theological but biological. The motivation for leaving didn't come from between his ears but from between his legs." Attempts at humor by making crude remarks reflected more of the mentality they were alleging than the reality of the situation.

From the start, I made up my mind that I would go through all the proper channels; follow all the proper procedures prescribed by Canon Law in seeking a leave of absence. For almost thirty years, my life was governed by the rules and regulations of the Passionists and the laws of the Church. I was not about to circumvent the law, a behavior, which I thought, would be scandalous and offensive in the eyes of all my friends. Following one's conscience, doesn't make the separation from life long friends easy, but hopefully, the mutual respect that existed for so long would remain.

As a Passionist, I followed the same monastic routine, shared the same meals, and enjoyed the companionship of some truly great and holy religious. Separating from these men would be very painful. They would be missed. The only thing I value more than the memory of these holy men is the prayers they promised for me upon my departure.

The Five Verity Boys (left to right: Harold, Gerard, Bud, Jack, and Bill)

Gerard, dressed for service as an Altar Boy

Gerard with younger brother, Harold

Frank Verity ("Pop") - the Fireman

Marguerite Verity ("Mom")

Gerard, 1939

Gerard at Holy Cross Seminary in Dunkirk, New York

Gerard, 1940

Gerard, 1941

Gerard, 1942

Gerard with older brother, Jack

Gerard, 1945

Gerard, at home in Laurelton, just prior to his trip to the
Novitiate

Gerard with Parents at LaGuardia, just prior to his trip to the
Novitiate

Gerard with his entire family at LaGuardia - the "Grand Send-off" (left to right: Harold, Jack, Pop, Mom, Gerard, Bud, and Bill)

Gerard at LaGuardia Airport, on his way to the Novitiate in
Pittsburgh, Pennsylvania

Gerard, now James, in the Novitiate

Jim, studying hard, in the Novitiate

February 27, 1953 - Ordination - Father James with his
parents, Frank and Marguerite

Father Jim

Father Jim teaching youth about the Passion of Christ

Father Jim administering the Eucharist to his parents

Father Jim celebrating Mass at Saint Gabriel's outdoor altar

Faithful volunteer, Cecilia McHugh

Jim and Ceil, "Newlyweds"

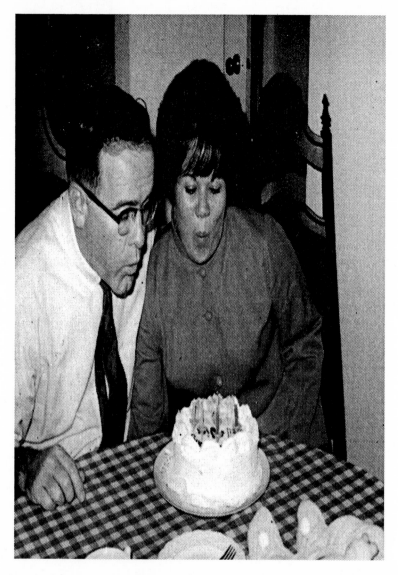

Jim and Ceil celebrating their first birthday together as a married couple

The Verity Family (Jim, Ceil, and their children, clockwise:
Jimmy, Sharon, Christine, and Eileen)

Jim and Ceil, 1998

Jim and Ceil, 2003

Chapter Twenty

I always knew that my life as a priest brought great joy and comfort to my parents and family. I was always there for them in their joy and sorrow – in marriages and baptisms, in hospitals, and at funerals. All this would come to an end when I took leave.

My parents were getting up there in years and I worried about their reaction to my decision to take a leave. Would Mom and Pop cry, have a heart attack, or what? I worried for them and it wore on me. I wanted them to be the first to know about my decision – no secondhand news from somebody else. I always remembered my mother's words twenty-eight years earlier when I first left home for Dunkirk, "This is your home. You can always come home if you're not happy."

When I finally told them of my decision, it was a replay of the same scene all those years earlier – the hugs, kisses, and all the emotion that goes into a life changing decision. For me, a great sense of relief also accompanied the sharing of this burden. Without any hesitation, my mother said, "Come home."

And Pop, standing by in silence but nodding in agreement, said it all when he threw his big arms around his wife and son!

What a relief! The three of us sat down for supper and shared plans for the future. When the meal was over, Pop donned his famous white apron, started washing the dishes and singing, "I love the flowers and the sunshine." Mom and I looked at Pop and smiled. It was as though I never left.

After supper, I contacted my four brothers and asked them to meet with me the following night. They arrived together and were unusually quiet. I guess they sensed something serious was afoot. Mom, Dad, my brothers and I gathered in the living room. I got right to the point and asked them to relay the message to their wives and children, all of whom I loved very much.

I then read to them the letter that I would be giving to all of my friends who were very supportive of me and the youth ministry we shared. After I informed my religious superiors of my decision, I planned to circulate the following message among my friends, both on Shelter Island and off.

Dear _____,

After countless prayers and many hours in the chapel, I made one of the most difficult decisions of my life. It is not a rash or hasty one. I will request dispensation from my Passionist vows and resign from the active ministry of the priesthood. I do so with a conscience at peace with God and myself.

I love the Catholic Church, the priesthood, and the Passionists deeply. I do not leave embittered, or disillusioned. My decision is strictly for personal reasons. I intend to remain fully united to the Catholic Church in my sacramental life. I am sincerely trying to love God now as I have always done so in the past. I have no qualms of conscience over my past priestly performance. With your prayers and help, God has blessed our ministry.

Those who are dearest to me, like my parents, who perhaps have the greatest reason to be upset by this decision, have been the most understanding. They are genuinely interested in my personal peace and happiness.

I tell you this for a number of reasons. By informing you directly, I want to avoid needless misinformation and speculation. Secondly, I want to urge you to continue to support the youth apostolate that we all love so dearly. Saint Gabriel's can go on without me, but not without you. It's God's work and He will continue to bless you for your part in it.

My immediate plans for the future are to live with my parents who have lovingly welcomed me back into their home – a home I left twenty-eight years ago to join the Passionists. Like Isaiah, I feel like a newborn in the palm of God's hands. I am starting a new life and I must trust in Him as I have urged others to do in far more precarious situations.

If I can face God in the choice I have made, I know I shall be able to face all of my friends. While you may not, at present, be fully able to understand my decision, I ask you to extend to me the same prayerful help I have accorded to the many who have come to me in the past, and that I would offer you were the circumstances reversed. God bless each of you and let's pray for each other!

Sincerely,
James Verity

As a group, all four of my brothers came over to me, shook my hand and offered their complete support. Things had not changed one bit between us.

Chapter Twenty-One

During this time period, I vividly remember phoning a religious superior to tell him that a priest friend of mine was absent without leave. I knew where he was and offered to help him. I was shocked and angered when the superior replied, "Forget about him!" This response was totally lacking in compassion and brotherly love. Unfortunately, this arrogant superior took another man's misbehavior as a personal affront. Is this an indication of why the Church has been referred to as "the only army that abandons its wounded?"

I went to my wounded friend and offered my help and support. He was grateful for the offer but too hurt and disillusioned by those who had distanced themselves from him. He never returned.

I wrote the Provincial a letter formally requesting a leave of absence. His immediate response was a phone call in which he first expressed surprise, which quickly turned to annoyance when he realized that this was no hasty decision on my part. He seemed more upset about the timing of the request than the request itself. I got the impression he was more concerned about the inconvenience this would cause him, due to the upcoming Provincial Chapter. He reminded me that I had been chosen as a delegate for the upcoming Chapter and asked me to delay my request until after. I told him that I could not, in good conscience, attend the Chapter and formulate policy or make rules for others to follow. This response, to say the least, was not well received.

Even though the Chapter was months away, the search for my replacement must have begun immediately because word about my request for a leave spread like wild fire throughout the Province and local dioceses such as Brooklyn and Rockville Centre. Phone calls and letters started to pour in from my friends in the Passionists and the diocesan clergy. I was deeply touched by a letter I received from Bishop Mugavero of the Brooklyn Diocese. He assured me of his constant support as a friend. He never forgot the help I gave to someone that he had referred to me for counseling. Bishop Mugavero was a good shepherd who wasn't about to toss one of his flock out to the wolves.

Other than during the summer, very few Passionists visited Shelter Island. Suddenly, I had a few unexpected visits from priests who were selected or volunteered to question me about my intention to seek leave. One priest, whose heart might have been in the right place, really got off on the wrong foot. To him, seeking a leave was tantamount to getting married. He believed that asking for a six-month leave was the equivalent of requesting a marriage license.

I can still hear his words, "Once you renounce your vows, you create a void and no person can fill the void that results from God's absence."

I answered, "I never equated a creature with the Creator. I never thought loving a creature and its Creator – or a human and God, were mutually exclusive. I can see no theological contradiction between the love of God and the love of my neighbor. As priests, you and I have extolled the sacredness of marriage, the sacrament of matrimony. After fifty years of marriage, I think my parents could teach you and me some lessons on how human love and the love of God complement and enhance each other."

I had a feeling that this interview was a fishing expedition, an attempt to find out my long-range plans. I reminded him that the purpose in seeking a six-month leave was to give me time to finalize my plans for the future. I assured him that if I were to seek a dispensation from my religious vows, I would go through the proper channels. And eventually, if I chose Laicization, I would petition it according to the norms set forth by the Holy See in Rome.

I told my visitor that I had as many different reasons for seeking leave as there were people making the request. This was not the time for over-simplification or generalizations. It should be a time for Church leaders and religious superiors to fearlessly ask themselves why more and more priests are seeking leave. It should not be taken as a personal affront. It wasn't as if I intended to betray the Congregation, leave the Church, or abandon my faith.

At this point, the conversation ended. My visitor had realized that my decision to apply for leave was final. I'm sure he communicated the outcome of our conversation to the Provincial once he returned to Union City. Until the formal leave of absence was granted, I continued the vigorous youth retreats and waited for the arrival of my replacement. During this waiting period, I made a lengthy tape recording of my reasons for seeking leave. My sole reason for making this recording was to share my own personal insights, hoping the Provincial and his assistants would be better prepared to guide others with similar intentions. The time and effort that I put into this recording would have been well worth it, if even one of my fellow Passionists would be helped by it.

A short time later, I was summoned to Union City for a meeting with the Provincial. When I arrived at Saint Michael's Monastery, I received a cold reception and was quickly ushered into a private room and informed that the Provincial would see me shortly. I certainly didn't expect a twenty-one-gun salute upon arrival, but I thought it strange that I should be isolated in a room for a few hours. The seclusion reminded me of the lepers of the past who had to alert the healthy population of their presence by crying out, "Unclean, unclean!"

When the Provincial finally burst into the room, his body language screamed that he was angry and impatient. His approach, if not his words, seemed to say, "Let's get this over with." He started off by telling me that he was very disappointed in me. He felt that it was inconsiderate of me to leave after so many of my fellow Passionists had elected me to represent them at the impending Chapter. Once again, he seemed far more concerned about himself and the inconvenience that my decision had caused. His first direct question was, "When do you plan to leave?" I told him I would leave once my successor was assigned to Saint Gabriel's and a smooth transition could be made. I had no intention of creating any problems for the retreat movement.

He made no comment, other than to tell me that I would be receiving $250.00 upon my departure. He asked no questions about how I would live or how I planned to survive. Before the meeting concluded, I told the Provincial about the tape recording that I had prepared and handed it to him across the desk. He raised his hand like a traffic cop, and simply said, "I don't want it." He stood up and without a handshake or a "goodbye," he abruptly left the room. The meeting was over. If there was any doubt in my mind or the slightest glimmer of hope that I would change my mind, the Provincial certainly threw cold water on it. This experience only reinforced my decision to leave.

I always thought that God, by giving us two ears and one mouth, was sending us a pretty obvious message that listening is twice as important as speaking. The Provincial was not a good listener, nor did he want to be. After fifteen years of faithful service as a Passionist priest, I was given an exit interview of less than fifteen minutes!

On my return to Shelter Island, I stopped off in Brooklyn to inform my faithful volunteer, Cecilia McHugh, and her family, that I was leaving the priesthood. During this short visit, my car was burglarized and the tape, which the Provincial had refused, became the property of a thief. So be it.

My final weeks at Saint Gabriel's were divided between the active ministry and preparation for my departure. Before my final Mass, in my favorite little chapel, I said farewell to all of my Island friends.

I returned to my parents' home to start a new life.

Chapter Twenty-Two

When I arrived home, I did not feel that I had abandoned God or that God had forsaken me. God's words to Isaiah (49:15-16) were very comforting to me during this period, "I can never forget you! I have written your name in the palm of my hand." The transition that I expected to be so upsetting, in reality, was calm and peaceful. To Mom and Pop, I was their son for whom they opened their hearts and the door to their home. It was as though I had never left. They were never ones to show off their son, the priest. After my thirty-year absence, Mom was simply delighted to have me back at the dinner table to devour her famous recipes. Pop was his usual self – the quiet giant who spoke with his eyes and a simple nod of his head. It was good to be home.

When I first left home, so many years ago, my youngest brother Harold was nine years old and my oldest brother, Bill, was twenty-one. When I returned, my brothers, their wives, and their children, reached out and welcomed me back. My brother, Bud, who was always a dapper dresser, became my personal haberdasher. He helped me select my first business suit, shirts, and ties. And when my $250 began to evaporate, he threw in a flashy pair of winged tip shoes. Bud said that my job search required two things – a good resume and a good appearance. At first, I was a little self-conscious dressed like a businessman. But as I rode the subway into Manhattan, I blended in with the crowd – just one more sardine in the cramped rush hour. I no longer stood out with my black suit and Roman collar and no longer received polite offers of seats.

The remainder of my dwindling cash supply was nibbled away by the subway turnstiles on my frequent trips into the city, in search of work. Were it not for my parents who fed and housed me, I don't know how I would have survived. I wanted to work; I wanted to be self-sufficient. However, the employment prospects were dismal. Going from a very successful ministry into the private sector was a radical change. Scouring through misleading want ads and following up on dead end leads left me exhausted and discouraged. A number of job interviews were granted by curious employers who seemed more interested in meeting an "ex-priest" than in offering me a job. I heard the phrase, "You're over qualified," more than I care to remember. Recruiters weren't clamoring for a middle-aged man with a theological background.

I tried not to lose heart in what seemed like an endless search for the right job. Starting each day off by attending daily Mass at the neighboring parish of Saint Mary Magdalene, reassured me that my life was still in the palm of God's hand. One day on my return home from morning Mass, my job search came to an end. The C.E.O. of Brothers Coach, Al Krpata, tracked me down and asked if I would work for him. His company had grown from a small family business to a six hundred-bus operation. He wanted me to inaugurate a Safety Program, which meant motivating drivers and dealing with insurance representatives and union officials. I would be a part of the management team, receive health insurance, a company car, and tuition reimbursement for any specialized training I sought. It was an answer to my prayer. Very quickly, the Krpata family accepted me as a team member and made my transition from the religious life to the business world a smooth one.

The first few months at home required a lot of readjustment. For thirty years, I shared my life with men whose basic religious beliefs and ideals were in harmony with mine. For the most part, we spoke the same language, with little room for disagreement. Now, I was speaking with men and women, management and labor, and people of all faiths and religious values. In the early days, I think some of my co-workers looked at me like I was from another planet. Their language was a lot more graphic and forceful than mine. At times, I found myself tongue-tied. Sometimes, when I suddenly appeared, their conversations would quickly halt or the topic would quickly change.

As an active priest, I never put on airs or acted holier than thou. I did not want to be a wet blanket or a kill joy. Years before, as a seminarian, I was fascinated by the "priest workers" in France who mirrored the image of Christ in their factories and marketplaces. Gradually, the language barriers disappeared, mutual respect developed, and new acquaintances grew into friendships. I never broadcasted that I had been ordained but somehow the priesthood always surfaced. This was the beginning of a whole new apostolate for me – the "priest worker."

The late 60's were difficult times for the Catholic laity. The old timers were upset with the rapid changes in the liturgy. The Latin Mass had a mystique about it and they missed it as it was phased out. The Latin Mass was the same in every parish around the world. The young Catholics adapted quickly to the changes but others were annoyed with the English prayers, the new hymns, the guitars, and the handshakes and kisses of peace. No two priests seemed to celebrate Mass the same. There was a lot of improvising. Liturgically, things were "topsy-turvy," but gradually, the old and the young, the traditionalists and the Vatican II Catholics were able to come together and worship in peace. Worshipping in the pews with the laity was an eye opener for me. I welcomed the changes and was only distracted by some of the extremes that took place in the sanctuary, as well as in the pews.

What started out as a tiny unpublicized trickle of priests and religious leaving the priesthood, was quickly turning into a mass exodus. This was a phenomenon that got the attention of the media and became one of the main topics of discussion in every parish and religious community. There were many stories of priests and religious who left and eventually married. There were also stories of others who left, but eventually decided to return. And there were front-page stories of Catholic priests who became Protestant ministers and pictures of married Anglican ministers who became Catholic priests. There were Catholic priests and religious who shocked the laity by leaving and others, that later scandalized the laity far more by staying. The laity was upset and confused.

It was during this period that I received a phone call at home from a representative from CBS news. I was asked if I would consent to be interviewed for the Walter Cronkite evening news, which would run on three successive evenings. The general topic was the increasing number of men leaving the priesthood. The setting for the televised interview would be my parents' home. I consented to do the interview.

To this very day, I cannot explain why I was chosen for this interview. I led a private life, was never in the limelight, was not a rabble-rouser, and wasn't in search of the spot light. I didn't have an ax to grind, nor did I have a prepared speech.

Ponchita, the interviewer, arrived with the television crew and all of their equipment. Very quickly, our dining room was transformed into a mini television studio. Ponchita joined my parents and me at the dining room table. She made her introductory remarks, as the camera panned the room and zeroed in on my parents and me. It all happened very quickly, leaving no time to get nervous. I had no notes, no outline, no make-up – it was very much a case of "what you see, is what you get!"

The interviewer got right to the heart of the matter. She asked all the questions that would capture the attention of the viewing public for three consecutive evenings. The following is a summary of the interview.

Interviewer: How do you explain the large number of men leaving the priesthood?

Response: I never anticipated that such a large number of men would seek leave. First of all, I can't speak for the other individuals who chose to leave. Each man has his own personal reasons for leaving. These men are not leaving the priesthood. They are resigning from the active ministry. It has always been the teaching of the Church that when the sacrament of Holy Orders is conferred, it remains forever – once a priest, always a priest. For example, if someone were in danger of death, or in a life threatening situation, the Church would still expect me to administer the Sacrament of the Sick and reconciliation.

Interviewer: Have you ever done this?

Response: Yes, a number of times, mostly at accident scenes on the highway.

Interviewer: What are your personal feelings towards the Catholic Church?

Response: I believe the Church has a divine origin, founded by Jesus Christ. From baptism on, I shared in the life of the Church. As a professional Religious and ordained priest, I served the Church wholeheartedly. Presently, I attend daily Mass, receive Holy Communion, and share the pews with the laity. In fact, when I formally requested my leave, I put in writing to the Vatican and my religious superiors in Rome, that I volunteered my priestly ministry locally and overseas as a self-supporting priest.

Interviewer: How did the Church respond to your offer?

Response: It didn't. A priest friend of mine said, 'Don't hold your breath or wait for a phone call.'

Interviewer: What are your future plans?

Response: I plan to work, earn a living and enjoy the company of my parents.

Interviewer: Do you plan on getting married?

Response: Yes. In a year or so, I would like to marry. Unfortunately, in the minds of some of the laity and clergy, the mere mention of marriage has a tone of finality about it. To some, marriage would be interpreted as the sole reason for resigning from the active ministry. This conclusion would be an oversimplification. Even more tragic, there are still those who think that the marriage of a priest is a divorce from God. No one is ever justified in passing judgment on another's ability to love God. There is nothing intrinsically or theologically present in the sacramental system that renders the sacraments of Matrimony and Holy Orders as mutually exclusive. Jesus, the founder of the seven sacraments, saw no conflict in appointing Peter, his married apostle, as the first Pope. The sacraments of Matrimony and the Holy

Orders are of divine origin, but the decision to make celibacy a condition for the reception of Holy Orders in the Roman Catholic Church is of human origin.

Do we have to wait until the Church is almost priestless before changes take place? Are the spiritual and sacramental needs of the laity of lesser importance to the Church than its opposition to optional celibacy for the clergy?

I will apply to Rome for permission to marry. Maybe if I live long enough, the Vatican will take me up on my offer to minister as a self-supporting, married priest.

When the TV crew packed up their equipment and left my parents' home, Mom, Pop, and I breathed a sigh of relief. It was good to be alone again. I said nothing in the interview that my parents had not heard before. I wasn't out to do any Church bashing. I only hoped that the interview would end any speculation by those who might have thought my relationship with God and the Church was in jeopardy.

Chapter Twenty-Three

I was into my leave for only a few months when I agreed to be interviewed for television. Up until that point, there were Passionists, diocesan clergy, and lay friends that were praying, and I am sure secretly hoping, that my final decision would be to return to the active ministry. The mention of my intent to marry during the interview, stirred up all kinds of conflicting emotions among old and new friends. Most of the repercussions were startling and unexpected.

Before the interview, my Passionist brothers sent kind and understanding letters assuring me of their friendship and support. There were phone calls assuring me of a "fresh start" should I decide to return. But at the mere mention of "marriage," an invisible wall was suddenly erected and the letters and phone calls stopped. The friendships that had developed and been nourished over the years, seemed to suddenly evaporate. I was incredibly saddened by this.

I didn't expect my decision to marry to be cheered. I could only hope that the love of my future spouse would not be interpreted as a rejection of my friendship with others. I sincerely hoped that time would heal these wounds. There's room in our hearts for all kinds of love and friendship.

In the late 60's, the whole Church, the dioceses and the religious communities, were hurting. Young candidates for the priesthood were no longer beating down the doors. New candidates were few and far between. There were more priests and religious leaving, than new candidates arriving. As the number of those remaining declined, their ministry to the laity suffered. The normal aging process, sickness, and death were relentless in the toll they exacted from the shrinking number of priests and religious. Contemporaries and classmates that I worked closely with in the past, were feeling the pain and strain of trying to heroically maintain the status quo. I felt sorry for them. They were struggling against a changing tide while the Church leaders seemed to have their heads in the sand. The feeble attempt by superiors to lower the standards for the acceptance of new candidates was not a long-term solution. The few who were responding to the call were not exactly a morale booster for those who governed their lives by much higher standards.

It was painful to stand by and watch all of this. And yet, although the number of priests leaving kept growing, the Church never even considered enlisting our help. An army of former religious and inactive priests was in reserve, ready to help. A lot of talent and goodwill was ignored. And why? Pride? Anger? Vindictiveness? Or was it a sense of betrayal that kept the Church leadership from seeking the great potential for good that existed among the former workers in the vineyard?

It almost reminded me of Custer's last stand at Little Bighorn. There's never a reason for an army to hold out until the last man when there are reserves standing by, ready, able, and willing to help.

In spite of all the turmoil and controversy brewing around the notion of a married priest or optional celibacy, the Roman Catholic Church will not self-destruct. It may suffer, it may be purged, and it may have to endure the pains of change, but it will survive. About eight hundred years before Jesus came on the scene, the prophet Isaiah said, "Fear not, I am with you. Be not dismayed, I am your God." And over two thousand years ago, at the Last Supper, Jesus reassured his apostles, "I will not leave you orphans."

It's God's Church, but the human element in it, from the top down, has certainly put it to the test. Dorothy Day often quoted Romano Guardini who said, "The Church is the Cross on which Christ was crucified." Those among the clergy and hierarchy, who vehemently uphold tradition and stubbornly resist any change to the priestly celibacy rule, are actually supporting the humans who broke tradition centuries ago. For Jesus ordained his apostles, without attaching celibacy as a condition for receiving Holy Orders. The most admirable people in the Church, today, are those who envision the future and are ready to change for what they hope tomorrow will be.

Does the Vatican fear that in making marriage optional there will be a mass exodus of celibate clergy? This is not likely to happen. Celibate priests won't be jumping out of the rectory windows in a mad rush to get married. Celibacy has its own rewards, its own comfort – and that is love. There are no mortgage payments, no need to provide a roof over your family's head. There are guaranteed three meals a day and the ultimate job security. The Celibate has only himself to care for.

Celibates must work very hard to be holy. The holier celibates become less encumbered in their love for God and neighbor. But the very freedom that celibacy is designed to create for loving God and his neighbor, can be devastating to the materialistic celibates who became more egocentric than theocentric, more parasitic than altruistic. Making celibacy a requirement for the reception of Holy Orders can be beneficial to the material needs of the Church, but historically, celibacy has not universally enhanced the image of the priesthood.

Any celibate priest who has done marriage counseling is well aware of the comfort and companionship that the human love in marriage creates. He also knows that human love is fragile and requires total attention and fidelity. From his own parents and former family life, a priest also knows that the happiness and satisfaction that come from a loving spouse and family, results from a proportionate amount of self-discipline and personal sacrifice.

I always believed that true friends help each other to be better people. During my fifteen years of active ministry, I made many friends among the laity. I was concerned about how my friends would react to the announcement that I intended to marry. I hoped they wouldn't be shocked or scandalized. I didn't want them to fear that my faith was in jeopardy or that I had turned my back on the Church. Some of my friends, who seemed to consider it a badge of honor to have a friend in the priesthood, felt rejected and sad. Unfortunately, some laymen get very possessive of their priest friends and interpret a shared friendship as a personal loss. Their shocking sense of loss was something akin to the reaction a person might have if they awoke one morning to find their prized car stolen from their driveway. It's a feeling of loss, shock, and disbelief.

Those friends, who were unhappily married, single, or divorced, couldn't fathom why someone as "free as a bird," would give up so much for so little. They were puzzled by my decision and would have been more agreeable had I chosen to become a single layman. I hope I never gave these friends the impression that I was so attached to the by-products of freedom and independence that celibacy offers, that I would resign from the active ministry in the lonely search for a care free lifestyle. I love people far too much to even consider that.

I was reassured by my friends who were happily married with children. In many different ways, they said they couldn't understand why priests were not permitted to marry. They thought marriage would enhance the ministry by giving priests a more balanced, realistic overview of matrimony – the love, the comfort, the self-sacrifice that grows with life long fidelity. They would understand the mixture of joy and total commitment that accompanies the birth and rearing of children.

Around this time, someone gave me a small, stained glass plaque that still rests on my windowsill today. I can't help but to see it every morning as I brew a pot of coffee. It reads:

> *"A friend is one to whom one may pour out the content's of one's heart, chaff and grain together, knowing that the gentlest of hands will take and sift it, keep what is worth keeping and with a breath of kindness, blow the rest away."* - Ancient Proverb.

Chapter Twenty-Four

Even though I was fortyish and had expressed the intention to marry, I knew it would take at least a year's preparation before it could actually happen. As an active priest, I met many fine, single women who, by worldly standards, might have been considered as good candidates for marriage.

As far as I was concerned, Cecilia McHugh was my first and only choice for marriage. In our many conversations over the years, Ceil never hinted, suggested, or asked that I leave the priesthood. Why was it that when a priest married, it was always the woman who was maligned? Ceil was not the evil woman lurking in the shadows, a temptress looking to lure the naïve priest away from God. For her, the priesthood was never an added attraction or challenge that made me more desirable.

In fact, her lack of respect for priests who treated the poor shoddily made her wary of anyone who wore the Roman collar! She didn't tar all priests with the same brush, but she certainly couldn't be counted among the laity who fawned in the presence of the clergy. She had a very sharp eye for any priest or religious claiming to be God's representative. Ceil's past history of volunteering in Church activities is proof positive that she was more interested in the mission of the programs than in those who directed them.

It was years later, that Ceil told me that one of the first things that impressed her about me was the ease I had in meeting her mother, brothers, and sisters. I took that as a great compliment. How could anyone put on airs in the presence of Ceil's tiny, Irish mother? A mother, who brought twelve children into the world, waged her own private war against poverty, and could still chuckle softly while sitting next to a visiting young priest. She was the hub of a large family, the centerpiece in that cramped little kitchen. I told Ceil that she need not be impressed with the man in the black suit. Instead, I was impressed with the gracious, little mother who sat next to me, put me at ease, and made me feel welcomed.

A few months after I got home, I was told that there was a rumor circulating around Shelter Island about why I left. People were gossiping that I left because I felt obligated to a woman who was riding in the front seat of my car with me and got seriously injured in a head on collision. I recalled a quote from Readers' Digest, "Nothing ever happens in a small town, but the rumors make up for it."

Ceil laughed at the rumor and remarked, "We should drive to Shelter Island and I'll put a pair of borrowed crutches alongside me in the front seat!" Ceil certainly wasn't the desperate little damsel waiting for the dashing knight in shining armor to scoop her up and carry her off into the sunset. If there were any chinks in my armor, she certainly was aware of them. Her astuteness in evaluating people always amazed me. I'm sure her early introduction into the business world, along with the survival lessons one must learn in the school of "hard knocks," made her a lot more knowledgeable in the ways of the world than I was.

It should come as no surprise that after twenty-eight years in a religious atmosphere, I had a lot to learn about the ways of the world. The religious life was not designed to make me worldly, just the opposite in fact. I did not have an insatiable craving for worldly goods, nor did I go hog wild in search of them. Being a celibate, living in a community of men, didn't turn me into a misogynist, but I could have used some instruction on the deferential treatment a gentleman should show a lady.

Ceil was very patient with me. It took a number of dates before I automatically stood back, held the door, and let Ceil enter first. Opening the car door for Ceil first, before I jumped in the driver's seat, did not come naturally. Fortunately, Ceil wasn't much on formality. However, with a few strategically placed "ahems" on her part, I was on my way to becoming a real gentleman.

Ceil had a clear, incisive mind that got right to the heart of the matter. She searched for the truth and when she felt she possessed it, she never hesitated to share it. When I first met her, I wasn't sure if she was cynical or just bitter in her observations about the Church. Her remarks and comments tested my patience and made me squirm on many occasions! A priest was not accustomed to being challenged by a layperson. Had they ever met, Ceil and Dorothy Day would have really hit it off!

Ceil thought it ridiculous that a priest would proclaim the fast and abstinence rules for the forty days of Lent, when her mother had to struggle to keep food on the table 365 days a year. Such comments reminded me of Saint Jerome's statement, "When the stomach is full, it is easy to talk of fasting." (342-420 AD). She could never understand how a priest could spend so much pulpit time asking the congregation to foot the fuel bill, when the Church and rectory were as warm as toast. In the meantime, Ceil and her family spent their winters trying to outsmart their stingy landlord. They used to place ice cubes wrapped in tinfoil on the thermostat so that the boiler would continue to pump heat up to the second floor. Some priests seemed totally unaware of the injustices and hardships inflicted on their poor parishioners.

Ceil could never understand or justify the invisible, man-made boundaries that separated the rich and poor parishes.

How could the Church tolerate these impenetrable boundaries that allowed some priests to say to the poor, "You have to go to your own parish?" Did Jesus restrict the distribution of the loaves of bread and the fish to those on the hillside who lived in nearby neighborhoods?

The human element was all too obvious among the clergy. I had to admit that, in my own life, there was a gap between what I preached on the pulpit and practiced in the street. I only wish the retreat masters who led our annual retreats would have been as insightful in their observations as Ceil was. Dorothy Day used to upset the Cardinals, Bishops, and priests with similar observations. Ceil's insight into the social doctrine of the Church made me examine my own conscience.

Ceil's personal relationship with God was secure and very private. She could relate to the Jesus who was born in the stable, raised in a carpenter's shop, and later on mingled in the marketplace with the blind, the hungry and the outcasts. He lived and died for what He believed in. Even as a young girl in parochial school, Ceil recalls how many times she heard the Sisters in the classroom and the parish priest say, "God loves you." She remembers saying to herself at the time, "If God loves us so much, then why doesn't He take care of my mother? Why doesn't He put some food on the table or mend the holes in our shoes?"

As a child, I never had reason to question God's love for me. As a boy, I pictured God as a kind, old man who was always looking out for me. As children, Ceil and I grew up in different worlds. The more I got to know Ceil, the more I realized how deep her faith in God really was. Even as a child, her relationship with God was put to the test and yet remained intact.

Without making excuses or denying the human element in priests, I tried to give Ceil a realistic picture of the men who wear the Roman collar. I told her to try to picture the young, idealistic priest, fresh out of the seminary. From the very first day that he reports for duty and moves into his private apartment in the rectory, his life begins to change in an almost imperceptible way. He has a roof over his head, he is served three square meals a day, and the cupboard is never bare. When he conducts his ministry, he dons beautiful vestments, enters an elaborately furnished sanctuary, and is listened to by a very respectful congregation. When the service concludes, he is greeted with smiles, handshakes, pats on the back, and lots of flattery, which if taken seriously can lull even the most sincere priest into a false sense of accomplishment. This adulation can take place in rich and poor parishes, week after week. It's a lifestyle that can slowly numb a priest and render him insensitive to the needs of his neighbors. Slowly and almost unconsciously, he can tune out the cries of the poor. Seeking the companionship of the problem free parishioners, can easily distract him from all the extended hands reaching out for help.

One day, I posed the following question, "Ceil, do you think it's easy for a priest today to maintain his ideals and be 'Christ-like'?"

She answered, "No, I don't. But he has to get out of the rectory. I can't remember the last time I saw a priest walk down my block. He should leave his car in the garage and wear out his shoe leather on the sidewalks of his parish. He preaches in the Church, but he should listen when he is in the street! His parishioners on the outside far outnumber those he reaches on the inside. When he first walks down the sidewalk, he will be seen as a stranger, as an object of curiosity. But slowly, over time, he will be recognized as a neighbor. After each successive visit, the image of the Good Shepherd will begin to become more apparent."

I couldn't argue with that.

Chapter Twenty-Five

My dates with Ceil were certainly not a yearlong series of discussions on pastoral theology or social justice. The more we got to know each other, the more we simply enjoyed each other's company. I think the fact that each of us was blessed with a simple lifestyle and a good sense of humor, diminished our need for outside entertainment or diversions. In the early days, we had very little money for wining and dining. Occasionally, we would stop in a "greasy spoon" luncheonette for a hamburger and coffee, but that was pretty much it. I would highly recommend these "walk and talk" type of dates for any couple trying to get to know one another.

I can't remember how Ceil and I happened upon the promenade in Brooklyn Heights, but it soon became our favorite spot. As we strolled along the promenade, we were treated to a spectacular view of the Manhattan skyline, the New York harbor, and the Statue of Liberty. On one cold night, a thin sheet of ice covered the promenade. As we strolled along, hand in hand, Ceil suddenly slipped and lost her balance. My attempts to keep her afoot were useless. She fell, landed on her back, and pulled me down on top of her. She laughed so hard at the startled look on my face and even harder when I accusingly asked, "What are you trying to do?" She kept laughing and squealed, "Your eyes are bugging out of your head!" I laughed, too. We got up, brushed ourselves off, and relaxed more than ever in each other's presence.

In very bad weather, we would seek shelter across the Brooklyn Bridge in Manhattan. We would take our usual place in one of the back benches of Night Court. We became part of a real cross section of humanity – sharing the benches with the observers and watching the accused appearing before the judge. It looked like a class in Humanity 101. Petty thieves, panhandlers, vagrants, prostitutes – a whole assortment of offenders were paraded before the judge.

On one wintry night, a poor homeless man was ushered in before the judge. The judge said, "Back again? It must be very cold out. Would you like a warm cell?" The man smiled, nodded yes, and the judge simply said, "You got it." As the old man was led away, he did a little jig and kept repeating, "Abracadabra." The court officers smiled, the poor man was given a warm place to sleep, and we left the courthouse counting our blessings.

One of the greatest blessings enjoyed by both Ceil and myself, was the genuine love and kindness extended to us by our families. I felt at home in the presence of Ceil's mother and family. And now, it was time for Ceil to meet my parents and family. It was only natural for her to feel apprehensive on her first visit. She worried about my mother's reaction because my Mom had always been so proud of "her son the priest." I reassured Ceil that my parents never tried to live my life for me. They were reconciled with my decision and only wanted me to be happy.

When I brought Ceil into the house, Mom was in the process of preparing a special, welcoming meal. Mom and Pop gave Ceil a warm reception and we all quickly relaxed. Mom and Ceil gravitated towards the kitchen, where Mom could keep an eye on the stove. When I heard a lot of chatter and laughter coming from the kitchen, I was very happy. I stayed with my father who was all smiles. It was obvious that Ceil was a hit.

Mom outdid herself in preparing a great meal, and kept saying to Ceil, "Don't be a stranger, eat more." A sure way to my mother's heart was to enjoy her cooking. Conversation during the meal came so easily that the two ladies remained seated, while I cleared off the table and carried the dishes to Pop, already draped in his white apron. He washed and I dried. I was so happy and relaxed.

When it came time to leave, Ceil kissed Mom and Pop. As I was about to walk out the door, Mom hugged me and said softly, "I like Ceil and feel very close to her already." On the way to Brooklyn, Ceil was very appreciative of the warm reception and welcome she received. I knew she would have no problems with future visits. All had gone well.

Following Mom and Pop's favorable reaction and their glowing reviews of Ceil, I quickly arranged a meeting between Ceil and my brothers and their wives. I was to bring Ceil to the Millbridge Inn, where the Verity clan would be anxiously waiting to meet her. Bill would bring my parents, Jack and his wife Ida would come in from Bayport, Bud and Peg from Melville, and Harold and Arlene from East Northport.

When I picked up Ceil in my trusty VW, she was extremely nervous. She didn't cherish the thought of being the center of attention. For some reason, she wasn't concerned about meeting my four brothers. From all of our previous conversations, Ceil felt as though she already knew them. I guess it was some kind of female thing that made her far more concerned about meeting my three sisters-in-law. They were well established in life, all married with children and living in their own homes. They had a lot in common with one another and Ceil was a newcomer.

I tried to reassure her that everything would be fine. I'm not sure that I was very convincing. I could sense how nervous she was and I felt for her. When we arrived at the Millbridge Inn, there sat the entire family, waiting for us and staring at Ceil. I pointed them out to Ceil and I empathized with her as she whispered, "Oh God."

Ceil went first to Mom and Pop and kissed them hello. She was then immediately surrounded by my brothers and their wives. There were no formalities. My brothers began clowning around and soon everyone began to relax. The ice was broken and Ceil's hearty, contagious laugh charmed everyone. There was no forced conversation or moments of awkward silence. I was very proud of her and very happy with my family for their kind and gracious reception of Ceil.

It was around this time that my official leave of six months was coming to an end. So, I wasn't surprised to receive a phone call from my old friend, Father Gregory Flynn, requesting a visit with me. The Passionists had every right to know what my decision would be – a return to the active ministry or a request for dispensation from my vows as a Passionist religious.

Ever since I first met Father Gregory, twenty-eight years ago when I entered Holy Cross in Dunkirk, I had always admired and respected him as a religious and priest. Over the years, he had become a close friend of the family. Not a year passed that he didn't visit my parents and enjoy Mom's cooking. When my thirteen years of training was complete and I was ordained, it was Father Gregory that I asked to preach at my first solemn Mass in Saint Clare's Parish. And now, he was returning to our home not knowing what the outcome of his visit would be. If he was nervous or upset with me, he didn't show it.

After a warm greeting by my parents and me, I introduced him to Ceil. She was friendly and at ease, which I'm sure helped him to relax. We settled back into the meal and he asked Mom and Pop about all of their grandchildren, etc. He never mentioned the true purpose of his visit – my plans for the future. He seemed to enjoy his meal, thanked my parents for their hospitality, and said goodbye to them and Ceil. I told him I would walk him to his car.

I sat alongside him in the front seat. He asked me what my decision was. I told him I wanted to be dispensed from my vows and that I planned to get married. I told him that I had given it much thought, prayed for guidance, and that my decision was final. I assured him that I would go through the proper channels and seek permission to marry from Rome. I also told him that I planned to volunteer my services as a married self-supporting priest, locally or in the foreign missions, if permitted. He didn't comment on this offer.

Father Greg told me that I was highly respected by the Passionists and that they would be saddened by my decision. With that, he reached under the front seat, pulled out some official documents, and asked me to sign my formal request for a dispensation. After giving my signature, we shook hands and I thanked him for his kindness and friendship over the years. He gave me his blessing and promised to send my request to Rome immediately. He kept his promise.

I am sure that Father Gregory was selected for this difficult task because of his longstanding relationship with the family and me. He did what he had to do and my respect and admiration for him never faltered.

When I reentered the house, I told my parents and Ceil of my request for dispensation and that Father Greg said he would handle it. Once again, Mom said, "Your happiness must come first."

Later that evening, as I drove Ceil home I told her what had transpired with Father Greg. I explained that my release from the Passionists was the first step and that afterwards I would be free to petition Rome for permission to marry. I also told her that I planned to offer to serve as a self-supporting, married priest.

Knowing this whole process was time consuming and realizing that I had no savings, I knew marriage was at least a year away. But still, it was time to pop the question. I stopped the car and asked Ceil, "Will you marry me?" I think I would have died if she had hesitated for even a moment. She didn't. She simply said, "Yes," and we sealed our plans with a hug and a kiss. From that moment on, we knew we would spend our lives together. There would be no more loneliness. Now, we had each other. It was a very happy and memorable moment.

Even now, as I recall my proposal, Ceil's spontaneity in accepting me as a lifetime partner, without any reservation, deepens my love and admiration for her. She had complete faith in me and fully supported me.

When I told her that I didn't have an engagement ring for her, she said, "Who cares! That's not important. I have you!" Next, I broke the news, "I have no savings," to which she responded, "That makes us even. I have none either." I finally reminded her that I had offered to serve as a married priest, possibly overseas. She laughed and said, "Well, I guess my new theme song will by 'I will follow him.'" She was completely optimistic and didn't even mind waiting the year. Ceil said, "Waiting one year to prepare for a lifetime together is a small price to pay. It takes three to make a happy marriage – you, me, and God. We can overcome anything. It was meant to be." I will always remember those words. Once I'd heard them, I knew for sure that we'd make it.

Chapter Twenty-Six

It wasn't long after Father Greg's visit to my parents' home that I received a phone call from the Chancery Office of the Brooklyn Diocese. I was finally invited to undergo Laicization. This was a formal process and the final step of separation from the active ministerial priesthood. In keeping with my intention to follow the due process of Church law, I requested an appointment for the first available date.

In the late 1960's, the word "Laicization" was becoming more common in the vocabulary of clergy. It was also creating more confusion in the minds of the laity. Newscasters and the media didn't help matters with expressions such as, "ex-priest," "defrocked priest," and "former priest." The Laicization process was compared to a court martial where a military officer was tried by his peers and, if convicted of a crime, stripped of his rank, dishonorably discharged, and relegated to a life of oblivion and disgrace. In actuality, a priest in good standing, guilty of no crime, but seeking permission to marry, was far more comparable to a patriotic soldier resigning from active duty and holding himself in reserve, should his service be required. I suppose it was more sensational for people to imagine the "defrocked" priest as one standing before his peers and having his Roman collar torn from his neck or his vestments stripped from his body in disgrace. This just did not happen; nor were we proclaimed as "former" or "ex" priests. At ordination, a priest is indelibly stamped with the priesthood and will remain a priest forever, according to the Church. The priest who is guilty of a serious crime in the eyes of a court, or a serious scandal in the eyes of the Church, is not the typical candidate who voluntarily seeks Laicization.

As I recall, I was quite nervous when I presented myself to the Brooklyn Chancery Office. Upon arrival, I was immediately put at ease by those who would take my testimony. There was nothing unpleasant or confrontational about the meeting. After a brief description of what was to transpire, I was led into what looked like a miniature courtroom. I was escorted to the witness stand and faced a priest tribunal across the room. I was informed that the proceeding would be recorded, transcribed, and forwarded to the Vatican for the final decision.

I would estimate that the whole session lasted about an hour. I was asked to describe my fifteen years of service as an active priest. When asked to describe my current relationship with the Church and my faith, I said, "I'm here seeking Laicization because I respect the laws of the Church and my faith has been kept very much alive by my attendance at daily Mass." There was nothing probing or embarrassing in their approach. The tribunal appeared satisfied with my responses.

After approximately a half hour, we took a short break during which one of the priests kindly offered me a cigarette. During this time, my fellow smoker asked me if I intended to get married. When I said I did, he suggested that I propose a definite date because it would expedite my processing in Rome.

The recorder was reactivated, the microphone turned on, and the testimony continued. I was asked if I planned to marry and I answered in the affirmative. The next question asked was about a wedding date, to which I responded, "May 24, 1969"- almost a year away.

The final question was, "Realizing the consequences of Laicization, are you freely and without duress seeking Laicization?" I responded, "Yes."

When the session ended, I was told that my request for Laicization and permission to marry would be sent to Rome immediately. I was assured that Pope Paul VI would not allow my petition to get buried on some secretary's desk or go unanswered. I would be notified as soon as the decision was made.

I was very grateful to the priests at my Laicization hearing. They transformed what had often been described as a dreadful experience, into an expression of genuine concern that had its roots in fraternal charity. At the conclusion, we shook hands and they wished me well. I thanked them for their kindness and I left the Chancery with a good, positive feeling. Now, it was just a matter of waiting.

Ceil and I didn't know if we would live long enough as a married couple to see the day when married priests would be reactivated in the ministry. But to this day, my offer to serve still stands!

Together, Ceil and I had a lot to accomplish in the following months and neither of us could or wanted to do it alone. Gradually, our manner of speaking was changing. The "I" was replaced by "we," and the "me" to "us." Love has a marvelous way of gradually melding together the minds, hearts, and souls of two individuals. Our plans for the future evolved into shared decisions and a common search for happiness.

As I returned home from work each evening, I checked the mail and asked my parents if there were any phone calls from the Chancery. It became a daily routine. Ceil and I, our parents, and our friends were all concerned about the Vatican's decision. We all felt as though we were in "count down" mode – the clock was ticking.

Ceil used to say, "Jim, don't worry about it. You followed the rules, took all the right steps, and went through all the proper channels." She reminded me of the story of the wedding at Cana. It was a human who fouled up the wedding of the poor couple, but Jesus came to the rescue. Ceil was certain God would come to our rescue as well. And she was right.

We had to make some down to earth, practical plans for our wedding. We wanted a private, simple wedding, nothing elaborate. Photographers, flowers, reception hall, etc., were all out of the question. It was to be a "no frills," bare bones wedding. Without neglecting our parents and our contributions to their household expenses, we pooled any savings we could manage from our modest salaries.

Ceil had spent her entire life in an apartment, being hassled by money hungry landlords. She deserved better, even if it were a two-room bungalow. This became our top priority. For Ceil, owning a home of her own was a dream beyond expectation. To make it a reality, we had to forego our talks and walks, and our trips to the Brooklyn Promenade. Our weekends, my lunch hours, and our evenings, were spent scouring neighborhoods and following up on real estate ads for potential homes. Even though we were very limited in what we could afford, we never wavered in our determination to find our own dream home.

While on a lunch hour at Brother's Coach, I did a random search in the "Five Towns" area of Long Island. I ended up in East Rockaway and spotted a "For Sale" sign in the front window of a small house at the end of a quiet street. It was shaded by large oak trees and surrounded by flowerbeds. The parish church, schools, and food stores were all within walking distance. It was a great location.

Mr. and Mrs. Carter, a retired couple, gave me a quick tour. The Carters were anxious to start their new retirement in Florida and wanted to complete a sale as soon as possible. I asked if I could bring my future wife back in the evening to see the house. They agreed. I guess Ceil could hear the excitement in my voice when I told her that I thought our search was over. She was thrilled.

The Carters were very kind and patient. They knew we were first time buyers and patiently answered all of our questions. As Ceil and I sat in the living room, a loud rumble outside suddenly startled us. We stopped talking and exchanged bewildered looks. The Carters quickly explained that the noise came from the Long Island Railroad, which just passed through the backyard on its way to Long Beach. They reassured us that it was basically a commuter line that transported workers to and from Manhattan in the morning and evening. The house didn't shake and no pictures fell from the wall, so we didn't worry about it.

When we returned to the house on Saturday to see it in the daylight, Ceil fell in love with it. Mrs. Carter was a "war-time bride" who had grown up on the English countryside. She obviously had a green thumb because our future home was surrounded by all kinds of spring flowers.

Jerry Perles, a lawyer who represented Brothers Coach, very kindly took us under his wing and guided us through the closing "pro bono." The house sold for $21,000. We took a twenty-five year mortgage at a 7.5% interest rate. With our combined salaries, we felt we could swing it. We became happy homeowners exactly one month before our marriage. During this time, I was dumbstruck by the spontaneous generosity of relatives and friends. Mom appeared with her paintbrushes and freshened up the interior trim of the house. Pop arrived with his famous plumbing bag and improved the piping. My brother, Bud, donated and installed a shower enclosure. My boss donated a lawn mower. And then, there were the bridal showers. Ceil's sister Betty, her co-workers at Schlitz, and even my boss' wife each gave her a separate shower. I didn't know what to make of all the gifts – linens, pots, and pans, dishes, and appliances. It was overwhelming. Like the poor couple at the marriage feast in Cana, what Ceil and I couldn't do for ourselves, others more than made up for!

Finally, after shopping and adding our own personal touches, our home was ready. We were on cloud nine. I recall feeling hurt when one visitor condescendingly commented, "What a cute, little starter house." As far as we were concerned, it was a palace – our palace. Only Pop, the man of so few words, was able to confirm what we already felt. When all the work was complete, Pop gathered up his plumbing tools, kissed Ceil, shook my hand, and said, "Your love nest is ready." He made our day!

Chapter Twenty-Seven

Months had passed since my visit to the Chancery and still no word from Rome. Time was running out. And once again, Jerome Perles came to the rescue. He knew our plan was to have a private wedding before a priest. Should the dispensation not arrive, Jerry lined up his friend, Judge Bernard Meyers to perform a civil ceremony. Once again, another stranger appearing out of nowhere to help us.

In preparation for a Catholic ceremony, we picked up copies of our Baptismal certificates – mine from Saint Martin of Tours in Brooklyn and Ceil's from the only parish in Queens named after a Passionist: Saint Gabriel's in East Elmhurst. It seemed Saint Gabriel was destined to play a part in both of our lives. When we compared our baptism certificates – we discovered something that we had somehow missed for all those years. We had both come into the world on the 14th of October! Of course, like any age conscious woman, Ceil was quick to point out that my October 14th birth had occurred ten years earlier than hers. I chuckled and this time, it was I who said, "It was meant to be."

As we slipped into May, we became increasingly anxious about the 24th. Each night after work, I would check the mail and look for phone messages – but still nothing. I was disappointed. We strongly preferred to receive the Sacrament of Matrimony in a Church before a priest. On May 23rd, I called Judge Meyers who assured me that he would be in his chambers on Saturday morning. According to our pre-arranged contingency plan, Ceil's sister Betty, as maid of honor, her husband Tony, my parents, and my brother Bud, who was my best man, were all to meet at the Supreme Court in Mineola.

When I arrived at Woodward Avenue to pick her up, Ceil was surrounded by her mother and sisters. She was all smiles. The only sad note of the day was that Ceil's mother, who was in poor health, would not be able to make the trip to Mineola in order to attend the wedding. I led Ceil downstairs, in her pretty white dress, and remembered to politely open the door to my VW for her. As we prepared to drive away, we looked up and there was her mother, smiling down from the window and waving as we pulled away.

When we arrived in Mineola, after the hugs and kisses, Mom, Pop, Betty, Tony, and Bud accompanied Ceil and me to the Judge's chambers. Judge Meyers gave us a warm greeting, donned his robes, and described the ceremony about to take place. In a very dignified and solemn way, he read a beautiful introduction before asking us to take our vows. It was a blending of a scripture asking for God's blessing and a prayerful reading extolling the sacredness of matrimony. He then asked us to exchange our wedding vows and then, calling on the powers vested in him by the State of New York, he pronounced us man and wife. The ceremony was done so reverently that I almost expected the Judge to give us his blessing and sprinkle our rings with holy water.

Judge Meyers said he was honored and happy to share in our joy. Then, seven very happy people enjoyed lunch at a little restaurant on Franklin Avenue. I'm sure it was one of the smallest and most modest wedding receptions that ever took place in Garden City. I'm also sure that it was one of the happiest. There was no music, no band, no flash bulbs, but it had all the elements of a marriage made in heaven.

After lunch, on our way to see Ceil's mother, we reviewed every detail of our wedding - the simple but reverent ceremony, the warmth of the judge, and the joy of our families. We marveled at how the details fell into place and how all the anxiety before the wedding had evaporated in the peace and love that surrounded us. Throughout the trip into Brooklyn, I caught glimpses of my bride extending her hand to proudly admire her wedding band. As we wove through the traffic, the smile never left my face. The new joy of Mr. and Mrs. Verity was abundant and mutual.

As we entered the apartment, Ceil's smiling mother, who was radiantly happy, greeted us. Everyone seemed to be talking and laughing at once. Ceil was showing off her wedding ring and excitedly describing the wedding ceremony. Without being evasive, we didn't describe our honeymoon plans except to say that we were going to Atlantic City. After a hug from my new mother in law, and a lot of well wishing, I escorted my new wife to our horseless chariot downstairs.

A few hours later, we arrived in Atlantic City and began our search for a reasonably priced hotel near the boardwalk. We found a Howard Johnson with a vacancy sign in the window. We got a simple room, not a honeymoon suite with a heart shaped tub! I'm sure the desk clerk probably assumed we were a couple celebrating their tenth anniversary, rather than their honeymoon!

After dinner in a quiet little restaurant, we took a stroll on the boardwalk. Walking hand in hand, oblivious to all others, and just being aware that we belonged together for the rest of our lives, made our relationship feel so right. Returning to our room that night was the perfect ending to a perfect day. Becoming two in one flesh was the most normal outcome in our love for each other. It was the culmination of all the goodness that attracted us to one another. It would have been blasphemous not to see the creative hand of God in all of this. If ever there was an appropriate time for Ceil to utter her famous words, "It was meant to be," it was just before we fell asleep.

While on our honeymoon, I phoned my old friend Joe Byrne whom I first met twenty-nine years ago on my first train ride to Holy Cross. Joe had been ordained a Passionist priest five years before me. He was now on leave and living close by. He and his future wife, Mary, joined us for dinner. They were obviously very happy together and a perfect match for each other. It was a very happy reunion – a lot of fond memories and many laughs. Joe and Mary wanted to hear all about our marriage, our home, and our plans for the future. As the evening came to a close, we all wished each other the best. Joe was a good religious and a fine priest. Together, Mary and Joe impressed us as great candidates for a happy life together.

As Ceil and I walked along the boardwalk, we agreed that it would be a terrible shame if the Church were to alienate a couple like Joe and Mary. As college professors, their potential for exerting a powerful Christian influence on campus was obvious.

Was the Church so blind that it could not, or did not want to, see the handwriting on the wall? What could justify the Church's refusal to harness such talent, to use the priestly services so desperately needed by the laity? What a shame! As the number of priests taking leave grew on the outside, the

Church officials on the inside kept busy by building a higher wall of separation. The dwindling numbers on the inside should not have felt threatened by the growing numbers on the outside. Hopefully, someday the flight of the Spirit back and forth over the man made wall, will inspire the priestly brothers to reunite in serving the faithful.

On our return to Howard Johnson, our little room was becoming claustrophobic, especially since neither of us could wait to return to our lovely, little home in East Rockaway. It was time to pack, load up our VW Beetle, and go home.

Chapter Twenty-Eight

For a few days at home, Ceil and I enjoyed our private life in East Rockaway. It was our intention to quietly blend in with our neighbors, not ashamed of my years in the priesthood, but not broadcasting them either. My anonymity lasted about three days. I was outside cutting the grass when a neighbor from the next block walked up to me and said, "Welcome to East Rockaway, Father James." She was very happy to have us as neighbors. She recognized me from the Jamaica Monastery, which is only twelve miles away. As the word spread, as it inevitably does in a small village, I worried that my priestly background might hinder our chances of fitting in. Thankfully, it did not seem to. Ceil had no problem making friends, both Catholic and non-Catholic. If there was any finger pointing, stares, or whispers, Ceil and I were too happy to notice.

A few days later, we received a visit from a priest and his wife. They lived nearby and had been recently married in a neighboring parish. Sadly, their description of their ceremony reminded us of a scene from "The Exorcist," where the priest walked down a dark, foggy passageway. In a similar setting, the couple was led by a priest into a dark, empty church. There, before a dimly lit altar, they pronounced their marriage vows. They were happy but felt sorry for the priest who seemed more concerned about maintaining the secrecy of the ceremony than emphasizing the sacredness of marriage.

Twelve days after our civil ceremony, Ceil and I were called into the Brooklyn Chancery Office. We could only hope that our sacramental marriage would be more dignified and reverent than this other couple's. God smiled on us – no darkness, no fog, and nothing spooky – just a bright, sunny day. Once we arrived, we were quietly ushered into a private office by a priest I met years earlier on a parish mission. In a very detached and business like fashion, he explained that Pope Paul VI had granted me laicization and permission to get married according to the Rites of the Roman Catholic Church.

Next, we were led into a tiny chapel, where behind closed doors, he witnessed us renew our marriage vows. Both of us were very unimpressed by the way the priest almost reluctantly conducted the ceremony. The wedding had none of the warmth or reverence that we had experienced twelve days earlier in Judge Meyers' chambers. At the conclusion of the ceremony, Ceil rushed to get out of the little chapel. She was rather uncomfortable and simply wanted to leave as quickly as possible. Unfortunately, she had not realized that the priest had locked the door behind us and she practically dislocated her shoulder trying to open the door!

Although it may not have been a pleasant experience, this ceremony was important to us. Should God bless us with children, we wanted them to be seen in the eyes of the Church as offspring of a Sacramental Marriage. For this, we were grateful. We received a marriage certificate, which read: "This is to certify that James Verity and Cecilia McHugh were lawfully married on the 5th day of June, 1969, according to the Rite of the Roman Catholic Church in the Parish of Queen of All Saints, as appears from the Marriage Register on file at this Chancery." It was signed by the Chancellor. However, it is on May 24th each year, that Ceil and I celebrate our wedding anniversary and thank God for each other.

One of the first things I did, when Ceil and I moved into Saint Raymond's Parish, was to inform the Pastor of our presence. I knew the pastor, Father Gerald Ryan, when he was stationed in a neighboring parish. I told him that I had no intention of going "public" but that, as a parishioner, I would be ready to help him in any way that he saw fit. He welcomed us into the parish and recalled the teenage retreats that I had given in Saint Agnes High School, a few years earlier. He asked if I would assist in his Religious Education program for public high school students. It was the start of a whole new life in the lay apostolate. Afterwards, Ceil volunteered her services as a teacher of a First Communion religious class. I am still grateful to Father Ryan.

Chapter Twenty-Nine

Ceil and I were hoping and praying for the blessing of children. It was the fall of '69 and we had been married for five months when our prayers were answered. I had been getting worried, and once again, was reminded that I should have had more faith and trust in God, the giver of life. As usual, Ceil came to the rescue and reminded me that it takes three to bring a child into the world, "You, me, and God." To Ceil, the hand of God was so obvious in our lives that she never doubted for a moment that God would hear our prayers.

Sure enough, she was right. It was in October, the month of our own births, that our child was conceived. Ceil was radiantly happy, I was overjoyed, and it was once again time for Ceil to say, "It was meant to be." Needless to say, waiting for the birth of our first child was the longest nine months of our lives. And yet during this period, our love for each other was enhanced and strengthened. Our hearts and minds became focused on the prospect of bringing a child into the world. A whole, new expansive love evolved through the process of procreation.

Our monthly visits to Doctor Kelly, in Far Rockaway, came to an abrupt end on the morning of July 17, 1970. Ceil went into labor and I rushed her to Saint Joseph's Hospital by 8 a.m. She was in labor for the next twelve hours, while I sat helplessly a floor below in the waiting room. I was so restless and anxious that I could barely sit still. Each one of the other prospective fathers had been summoned up to the maternity ward to see their wives and newborn children. A whole new shift of nurses and security guards came on duty. I was alone and pacing back and forth. The security guards seemed to take turns peeking at the middle-aged man pacing the floor. Finally, the doctor came down and said there had been complications and that he might have to do a "c-section." My heart stopped but I told him to do whatever was best for my wife and our baby. The phone rang a half hour later and the doctor said, "Congratulations! You have a daughter and both she and your wife are fine. There was no need for the c-section. Come see your family!"

As I rushed off the elevator at the maternity ward, there was an elderly nun sitting at a desk. She looked up and said, "Good evening, Father" and then quickly put her hand over her mouth, realizing that the wrong words had escaped. I wasn't sure if she had recognized me and was now confused by my presence and the lack of the Collar. Obviously, I didn't have time to inquire. However, when I saw her afterwards, she said, "I'm sorry. You just look like a priest and I automatically called you Father." Although we'd never met before, the nun simply saw something familiar in me. I responded, "Don't be sorry, Sister. I am a priest and now a father. So please, from now on, feel free to call me 'Father Father.'" The nun laughed and for the remainder of her stay, I think Ceil received extra special care and attention!

Ceil went through a very difficult labor but came through it fine and in great spirits. My tiny daughter, Sharon Ann, was so beautiful that my eyes kept darting back and forth between her and Ceil. I can't describe the happiness and joy I felt. In my own heart, I continuously thanked God for watching over Ceil and for giving us a daughter. Ceil was so right when she said, "It takes three to bring new life into the world – you, me, and God." God's presence was felt very strongly as we gazed upon the gift of life which we were privileged to bring into the world. The creative hand of God is never more apparent than at the birth of a newborn child.

It was an extremely happy time – a unique happiness that only a newborn brings to its parents. I remember one evening after supper, very clearly. While Ceil was busy in the kitchen, I was in the living room cradling Sharon in my arms. We were both very relaxed when her tiny hand reached up and wrapped itself around my little finger. I can't describe, nor can I forget, the joy that welled up within me, except to say that I couldn't hold back the tears that rolled down my cheeks. Unknowingly, my tiny daughter was melting her father's heart. The Creator was setting in motion a whole new form of love – parental love.

All of Ceil's motherly instincts came naturally. Feeding, holding, changing, and bathing came very easily to the new mother. While I was a little awkward at first, I was surprised to see how quickly I learned the rudiments of being a father. Actually, I couldn't wait to get home from work to be with my wife and baby. A tiny, helpless newborn that is totally dependent on her parents for survival has a unique way of not only changing the lives of two adults, but also has a marvelous way of strengthening the bond of love that unites them.

This lifestyle transformation is not unique to us humans. Outside our home, we have a bird feeder as well as a few homemade birdhouses in the trees. During the winter, my favorite little sparrows act like nasty little street fighters as they selfishly gobble up the seed from the feeder. Survival of the fittest seems to be the dominant instinct. They push and peck at each other in their struggle to fill their stomachs.

When spring arrives, they pair off, take ownership of the houses, mate, and work as teams to build nests and hatch their eggs. Then, from dawn to dusk, the mother and father are totally dedicated to satisfying the voracious appetites of their offspring. Finally, the excited singing and chirping of the parents announces to the world that their fledglings are prepared to take flight. We humans, who like to think of ourselves as the crowning glory of God's creative work on Earth, can learn some powerful life lessons from our little, feathered friends.

The day of Sharon Ann's baptism was a very happy one. After a beautiful ceremony at Saint Raymond's Church, we returned home to a house filled with family and friends. There were lots of hugs and kisses, smiles and laughter, food and drinks. After all of our guests departed, Ceil and I had Sharon to ourselves. We were grateful to God, our families, and our friends, but mostly to Sharon Ann who was the greatest source of our joy.

Ceil was usually at the front window looking for me, as I pulled into the driveway from work. On one particular evening that next September, Ceil had Sharon in her arms and was waiting with the door open. It was as though she couldn't wait for me to enter. She was all smiles and radiantly happy. After I kissed her and Sharon, she blurted out, "I'm pregnant!" The instantaneous joy I experienced at this announcement was no less intense than the happiness that filled our hearts eleven months earlier at the news of Sharon's conception. A few days later, we were back in the doctor's office when he predicted that our second child would arrive in mid June 1971.

Unlike the long wait for Sharon, I hardly got Ceil into Saint Joseph's Hospital when I was called into the maternity ward. After informing me that both mother and daughter were doing fine, the doctor said, "You know, for a former man of the cloth, you sure are making up for lost time!" I laughed and said, "Let's hope it won't be too long before we see you again!" He slapped me on the back and said, "God bless you." I responded, "Thanks but God has blessed me and my wife more than you can imagine."

My beautiful Eileen Mary arrived on June 15, 1971. I couldn't wait to take Ceil and Eileen home. We wanted to show Eileen off to her sister and our friends and family. Our small home was beginning to look and sound like a nursery. The washing machine never stopped. The clothesline sagged under the weight of drying diapers. Ceil was as busy as a one arm paperhanger. She quickly improvised and got the care of her babies down to a science.

Between cribs, carriages, and baby furniture, space was a premium. The family was growing and the house seemed to be shrinking. It was time for expansion. For the next year and a half, with my trusty circular saw and a few basic tools, I began to finish the basement. Money was tight, but stud-by-stud, panel-by-panel, empty space was becoming living space. Through my weekly shopping trips to the lumberyard, with lots of guidance from the salesmen, I was slowly developing from a wood butcher into a decent carpenter. During my seminary years, I remember reading a passage about "the beautiful hands of a priest." Recalling that quote, I had to smile at my hands, now calloused, cut, covered with splinters and blood blisters. They weren't very beautiful but somehow I thought they might resemble the hands of Joseph the Carpenter and that suited me fine.

Towards the completion of the basement, Sharon learned how to back down the stairs on her knees to be with her father. Whenever she arrived, all work would stop. The electric saw had to be unplugged, the box of nails closed. I enjoyed the change of pace as the two of us would sit on the floor and play in the sawdust. Pretty soon Ceil would join us with Eileen in her arms and we'd all draw smiley faces in the sawdust. Those were great days. I wish they didn't fly by so quickly.

Carpentry took up most of my evenings and a big portion of my Saturdays. Sunday was our family day. After Mass, weather permitting, the four of us would pile into the VW and go for a ride to escape cabin fever. Sometimes, it was a short ride to Baldwin to feed the ducks. Other times, we'd drive to the seashore to build sand castles. These trips forced Ceil and me to become expert space savers. We occupied every square inch of our little VW Beetle. The back seat was transformed into a little nursery for Sharon and Eileen. Milk, baby food, baby powder, diapers, etc., were stacked in the back seats to take care of the girls. Sandwiches, pretzels, and sodas were stashed up front for us.

Once, after Labor Day and in the off-season, we were able to afford to rent a little cabin in Hampton Bays. It was primitive – no radio or TV, just a tiny stove and a no frills kitchen and bathroom. It was only a step away from real camping. We had the place to ourselves. It was deadly quiet – no planes overhead, no cars, and no trains – just the fall leaves bouncing around in the steady breeze off the bay. The silence reminded me of Shelter Island, but for Ceil, the city girl, it was a new experience. I remember her waking me up in the middle of the night and saying, "Jim, it's so quiet. Would you check the babies to see if they're breathing alright?" I did and found them just fine. I told Ceil to "relax and go back to sleep." I talked to her about the outdoors, the strolls on the beach, the building of sandcastles, and the collecting of seashells – all the ingredients Mother Nature uses to lull babies into restful sleep. The words were hardly out of my mouth when Ceil joined her daughters in slumber. I smiled to myself as I lovingly gazed on my three sleeping beauties.

I'm glad that God could hear the silent prayers of Thanksgiving that filled my heart in that little cabin. I soon joined my family in a deep, peaceful sleep.

Chapter Thirty

As a seminarian, I was very interested in the Church's social doctrine. It was one of the best-kept secrets. I admired the few priests who were involved in the labor movement, and the members of the laity, like Dorothy Day, who championed the needs of the poor. I always found myself siding with the poor, the down trodden, and the migrant workers. I always thought that "a fair day's work, for a fair day's pay" was a common sense guideline for both worker and employer.

In Europe, the Priest workers who shared the workbench and production line with the factory workers, were attempting to bring the message of Christ into the workplace. But as a seminarian, a religious, and a priest, the workplace had remained a distant world where I found myself outside, looking in. It was impossible to fully understand the boredom of a dreary, monotonous job. I never punched a time clock nor was I ever subject to a boss whose idea of justice was totally self-serving and diametrically opposed to any sense of fairness.

In 1969, I embarked into the world of the worker. The transition was not easy. I had a lot to learn from teachers, both good and bad. My co-workers were a mixture of saints and sinners. I was living on a razor's edge, trying to maintain a prudent balance between upholding my ideals and not alienating those who had a different lifestyle. My introduction was a mixture of a learning process, a school of hard knocks, a rude awakening, and occasionally, it was a barrel of laughs. But it's amazing how adaptable we can be when our ability to put "bread on the table" depends on it. Preaching from a pulpit to a silent congregation was far less challenging than preaching by example to vocal co-workers.

My first job was with Brother's Coach, the same bus company that had transported the teenage retreatants to Shelter Island. Through the efforts of an entire family, Brother's Coach became one of the largest transportation fleets on Long Island. I was trained to run the Safety Department. It was a great job, which gave me direct access to hundreds of employees, their union, management, and insurance representatives. After a few years, for reasons unknown to me, I saw this thriving operation quickly crumble and go bankrupt. The owners, who formerly were generous benefactors of Saint Gabriel's, were now concerned about their own families and saving their homes. To witness this breakup of a family venture was a very painful experience, not only for the owners but also for the hundreds of employees. For me, the saddest part was my inability to help this family that had always been so good to me.

There was hardly a break in time between the loss of one job and finding employment in another. I received a phone call from a very wealthy man who had invested heavily in a Brooklyn bus company. He said that I came highly recommended as a person with a great deal of integrity. In his own words, he was looking for a "few good men who could keep their noses clean." A retired marine colonel and I, were called into New York for interviews. We were both hired.

When I arrived on my new assignment, I felt about as welcome as a skunk at a lawn party. Obviously, local management knew that I had been assigned by the main office. It was a rinky-dink operation with a lot of shenanigans going on. The union workers were unhappy and had no respect for management and management had done little to earn their respect.

When the president of the Transport Workers Union saw me and remembered me from Brother's Coach, he said, "Jim, what are you doing here? You're like a bar of ivory soap in a cesspool!" It was a sinking ship. To remain, would have been to condone the corruption and thievery. I wasn't about to compromise my good name and reputation. I tendered my resignation. As anticipated, following an investigation, the whole operation was shut down.

For the next few weeks, I stood on line with the army of the unemployed and collected checks from the New York State Department of Labor. Unemployment checks don't go very far. They barely manage to put food on the table and pay a few bills. Slowly but surely, the small savings that we had put aside, began to evaporate. It was a time of tightening the belt and pinching pennies.

As an active priest, I used to tell others in similar circumstances not to lose hope and to put their faith in the hands of a provident God. Now, it was my turn to worry about my wife and children. I soon learned that it was a lot easier to preach about the virtue of hope than to practice it in the absence of a paycheck!

On my visits to the unemployment office, I was saddened by some of my unemployed companions when they shared their horror stories about the working conditions of their former jobs. Most of us were embarrassed to have to stand in line and take a handout from the State. Many were frustrated, angry, and desperate. They felt they were on a downward spiral into poverty. I could empathize with them - just like me, they were unemployed through no fault of their own.

Going to the unemployment office was an eye opener for me. I mingled and stood on line with a cross section of unemployed American workers. For those of us who really wanted to work, these sessions at the unemployment office took a toll on our self-esteem. Those on line who were working the angles and milking the system were the exception.

My weekly trips to the unemployment office ended when I was offered a job in the Holmes Ambulance and Medical Supply Company. It was a small family-owned business located on Flatbush Avenue in Brooklyn. It was an easy transition. The owners and two priests, already hired, welcomed me aboard.

It was suddenly 1973, which turned out to be a very good year for all of us. In March, Ceil gave birth to our third daughter, Christine Cecilia. Once again, God blessed us with a healthy child. Ceil and I couldn't thank God enough for the privilege of bringing new life into the world. The only way we, as parents, could fully thank God was to treasure, care for, and raise our newborn to the best of our abilities.

When I walked into the maternity ward and saw Ceil with Christine in her arms, both seemed so relaxed. Ceil was all smiles and Christine was sound asleep. When Ceil handed me Christine to hold for the first time, she remained asleep in my arms. Was it because we were more relaxed as "third-time" parents, that our newborn felt more secure in our presence? It occurred to me from that day on; each child, in its own unique way, begins to react to the vibes we parents radiate. As I gazed at my sleeping daughter, I was wondering if her silent contentment was her way of expressing the comfort she felt in my arms. When Christine arrived home, her ability to sleep straight through the night was a gift that Ceil, her two sisters, and I really appreciated!

If I remember correctly, it was the old Irish Sister in Saint Joseph's maternity ward who said, "Remember Jim, every newborn child comes into the world with a loaf of bread under its arm!" She was so right. I guess the loaf under Christine's arm was a phone call I received about a month after her birth. Isn't it mysterious how people from our past can suddenly resurface just at the right time to profoundly impact our lives? This time it was Justine Sugrue, whom I'd met five years earlier on Shelter Island. At that time, she was Sister Justine of the Dominican Nursing Sisters. She and her Dominican companions impressed me very much in the care they gave to the sick and poor of Eastern Long Island. Now, Justine was married to Jim Sugrue, a former diocesan priest who served the poor in Manhattan.

At the time, Jim Sugrue was employed by United Parcel Service (UPS) and served as the Human Resource Manager for the Long Island District. While Ceil and I were visiting Justine and Jim, he suggested that I apply for a position with UPS. I took his advice, joined UPS, and worked there until my retirement, fifteen years later. It didn't surprise me that God continuously chooses people like Justine and Jim to put themselves out to help others. People who love people are never idle – God always has someone in mind for them to help. Once again, the help Jim and Justine provided to me was "meant to be."

It was in April of 1973, that I went to the UPS employment office in Maspeth, New York. As I entered the building, there was a sign above the entrance that read, "Our people are our greatest asset." It was a positive message and let me know that the company valued its employees. So far, so good. I was excited about the prospect of joining such an organization.

When I entered the employment office, I was handed an application and ushered into a room filled with twenty year olds. I was in my late forties, old enough to be the father of anyone of them. The man who interviewed me was a brusque, blustering individual who gave me the impression that this was a courtesy interview and that I had little chance of getting hired. The only glimmer of hope was a poster that I noticed on the wall. The poster stated that it was illegal to discriminate against applicants between the ages of forty to seventy. The fact that I was the only gray haired applicant in the room, might turn out to be an asset rather than a liability, for a company intent on practicing affirmative action. Subject to passing a physical exam, I was given the green light and told that I would be notified of when to report to work. I'm sure that my previous experience as a fleet safety director was also a contributing factor in their decision to hire me.

I received a phone call after passing the physical and was told to report to Walter Borys of the Safety Department. I thanked Jim Sugrue and assured him that I would do my best. The Safety Manager was a highly dedicated and respected employee who took me under his wing. He was the living embodiment of the UPS spirit, someone who, as the company saying went, had "brown blood." He was a mentor and taught by example.

For the next fifteen years, I worked in all different departments of Human Resources – safety, employment, the employee assistance program, etc. My assignments were almost equally divided between night shifts and day shifts. In spite of the drastic changes in lifestyle that night work demanded, I managed to enjoy most of the work. The effort to adapt was well worth it. I enjoyed rubbing elbows with the night crews – the hidden UPS-ers. They were the people who worked behind the scenes, away from the eyes of the public. They were teamsters who worked feverishly throughout the night - unloading trailers, sorting parcels, and loading the brown delivery vans for the drivers who would spend the daylight hours delivering the parcels to customers. The whole night operation was highly organized and called for a lot of teamwork and cooperation between labor and management. It took me a while to fully understand all the intricacies of the gigantic hub operation in Maspeth.

The night workers were a cross section of humanity – a multi-cultural mix of all races, nationalities, and creeds. Most were veterans, a few from World War II and the rest from Korea and Vietnam. What I liked most about these rough and tough workers, was the way they spoke their minds. They were direct; there was no sugar coating – they left little doubt about what was on their minds. When they spoke or shouted, their message was clear, "What you hear, is exactly what I mean." I found it refreshing.

When I was a boy the worst curse word one could utter was the "f-word." On the night shift, the f-word had a million variations and I slowly learned them all. It was a noun, a pronoun, a verb, an adverb, and an adjective. It expressed joy, sadness, disappointment, anger, and pain. Sometimes, I thought their spicy language was exaggerated for my benefit. In the beginning, it was hard to keep a straight face but after awhile their colorful language made me smile, laugh, frown, or even nod my head in agreement – depending on the message. Even though the lack of the f-word in my vocabulary must have made me sound like an alien, we all really enjoyed each others' company.

A big part of my assignment as a Human Resource representative was to sit down, one on one, with the employees and allow them to comment about anything related to their job. With permission from his boss, I was able to take the night worker away from the job site to some suitable place where he could speak freely over a cup of coffee. If he had a serious complaint about anything or anyone, I assured him corrective action would be taken without retaliation. Following up on a justified complaint was like stamping out a spark before it turned into a roaring inferno. If the employee had positive suggestions about his job, they would be taken seriously. Once word spread that these talks produced positive results and that I could be trusted, these sessions became very productive and rewarding.

At the conclusion of one talk, a night worker said, "Thanks for listening. I've been bothered by this for a long time and it feels great to get it off my chest. You remind me of a chaplain that I used to speak to in the service." I doubt that employee ever knew how much those words meant to me.

One morning, about 3:30 a.m., I was car-pooling home with my friend, Russ. He was a jolly guy with a great sense of humor and a contagious laugh. About half way home, he was almost apologetic when he said, "Jim, I don't know how to ask this, but what makes you different? You don't yell, scream, or curse. You're kind to everyone. How come?" His observations made me laugh. I had never seen him so serious. I told him that I was going to share something with him that I didn't want him to advertise. I told him that I was a priest. He was so surprised and excited that I feared he would lose control of the car. The information I shared with him led to many good conversations and in no way put a damper on his lively sense of humor. I was grateful for that.

While I never bragged about or flaunted my life as a priest, my past slowly seeped out. Knowledge of my background actually improved my rapport with the workers, the teamsters union, and management. When I was asked to pilot an Employee Assistance Program, my boss told me that I was selected because both management and labor knew that I was trained to keep secrets. Each time upper management or the president of Local 804 asked me to assist an individual in need of help, I found that the absence of the Roman collar made no difference in my ability to do so.

There were two outstanding incidents that touched me very deeply as an inactive priest in the work environment. The first was when a worker collapsed on the job from serious heart failure. Because I was a priest, I was summoned over the public address system to comfort a dying co-worker. I was able to kneel on the floor along side of him and give him absolution. He died in the ambulance on the way to the hospital.

When I informed his wife that I was able to give her husband absolution before he died, she was very grateful. In her eyes, I was more than a co-worker; I was a priest who was with her husband in his final moments. To her, that was all that mattered.

The absence of a black suit or Roman collar did not prevent her from recognizing me as a priest.

The second experience to profoundly touch me, took place on the night shift in the Maspeth Hub. When the lunch period started, the massive workplace became quiet. Electric motors were turned off, conveyor belts stopped, and hundreds of workers bee-lined to the cafeteria. Unknown to me, and I'm sure to many of their co-workers, a handful of workers would gather quietly in a small room, not much bigger than a closet. After finishing their lunch, they would spend the remainder of the lunch hour in quiet reflection. I felt honored when this small inter-faith group invited me to join them.

When I entered their tiny, unadorned chapel, these sincere men were kneeling on the concrete floor, praying in silence. They had a brief discussion of a scripture passage and then returned to their work stations. I was deeply impressed and the passage of scripture that entered my mind was, "Where two or three are gathered together in my name, there am I in the midst of them."

Is it a surprise that my co-workers saw no conflict between the priesthood and marriage? On the contrary, the combination of the priesthood and marriage seemed to close the gap between the priesthood and the laity. To the men of UPS, I was different and yet the same. It was a hidden ministry that came to the surface each time a priest was needed but couldn't be found.

Chapter Thirty-One

It was usually Saturday evenings following supper and after the girls were tucked in bed, that Ceil and I had our best conversations. We never held anything back from each other. There were no secrets, no subterfuge. There were the discussions and the disagreements that are a part of every marriage. We both shared time wearing the pants and the apron.

It was during one of these quiet chats in '74 that Ceil said, "Jim, I think it's time for us to open our home and share our blessings with a poor child. I think we should check out adopting a child." Ceil's suggestion didn't really surprise me – after all, she loved children, had a special place in her heart for the poor, and an incredible spirit of generosity. Our little house was already much like a nursery with our oldest of three daughters not yet even four. I asked Ceil if she could care for another child. She gave me one of her famous, "Are you kidding?" looks and answered, "Of course!"

Once more, my love and admiration for my wife grew by leaps and bounds. The joy, the anticipation, and the excitement that comes with the prospect of having another child was overwhelming. We sealed our intention to adopt with a hug and a kiss.

On the next day, Sunday, we piled the girls into the car and drove into Brooklyn to visit the Angel Guardian Home. It was the adoption agency conducted by the Sisters of Mercy. Neither Ceil nor I had any idea of what was entailed in adopting a child. The Mercy Sisters were very kind and hospitable. We were told, when they saw our three daughters, that childless couples were given preference in adoptions. We agreed with this policy wholeheartedly. The Sister also asked us if we had any preference for the child in terms of gender, race, age, etc. Ceil answered that we would leave that in God's hands, as He had already blessed us with three healthy children. We reassured the Sister that the door to our home would be fully open to any child that might need a home.

The interview seemed to go well. The Sister did not go into details about our health, age, home, or income. She said she would arrange for a social worker to do a follow-up home interview. When asked how long the adoption process takes, the Sister refused to give a specific answer but she did warn us that it often took longer than the nine months that we had waited for each of our daughters.

The first thing we did when we settled back into the car for the return trip home, was to review the interview. We recalled the Sister's words, the expression on her face, her favorable comments about our children, etc. As we pulled away from the curb, we were hopeful and encouraged by the assignment of a social worker for a home visit.

A week later, the social worker arrived at our home. She was kind and understanding but also thorough and professional. She did a walk-through of our home and told us that a private room would be required for an adopted child. We assured her that this requirement would not present a problem. This was the first of a number of home visits. Obviously, the Mercy Sisters took their responsibility as Guardians very seriously. The Mercy Sisters, standing in for God and Mother Nature, were most careful in selecting parents for the children entrusted to their care.

It was almost a year later, while I was working the night shift at UPS, that Ceil received a call from Vietnam. A Mercy Sister said she had brought fifty applications for children to Vietnam, in response to President Ford's "Baby Airlift." She said that the fifty applications had been reduced to four and that we had been selected as one of four prospective couples. She selected a little four-year-old boy from an orphanage in Saigon. He was what she called "Amer-asian," dark skinned, racially mixed. He was to be flown out of Vietnam on the Baby Airlift. Ceil called me and we both agreed that this was an answer to our prayer. Ceil called the sister and it was confirmed. Our son,

Tran Van Mingh, was to arrive at LaGuardia Airport on April 9, 1975.

Ceil, the girls, and I were at LaGuardia well in advance of the plane's arrival. When we got to the gate where the children were to disembark, Cardinal Terence Cooke, many dignitaries, and members of the media with their TV crews and flashbulbs, were there to welcome them. Excitement mounted as the plane came to a stand still. As the first orphan was escorted down the ramp, the Cardinal, the dignitaries, and the media tightly encircled him.

All of the children had identification tags around their necks and wrists. As one child after another descended from the plane, the crowd cheered. It was a very emotional event. Ceil was getting frantic; she feared that the crowds would prevent her from being at the front of the ramp when our son disembarked. I offered to watch our daughters so that Ceil could make her way to the front and claim our son. I was proud of her as she elbowed her way through the crowd. I don't know if the children were escorted off the plane alphabetically, but finally, a little four-year-old boy exited the plane and was introduced as Tran Van Mingh Verity. Ceil was right there to scoop him up and hug him. Flash bulbs were popping all over the place. The long wait was over. Soon, our son would be at home with his new Mom, Dad, and sisters.

On the way out of the airport, we stopped at the TWA ticket counter and told the agents that we were prepared to pay the airfare for our son but did not know if we had enough money. They smiled and said, "There is no charge." Ceil smiled, looked at me, and her eyes seemed to say, "It was meant to be."

Our new son couldn't speak a word of English and, of course, none of us knew a word of Vietnamese. We were very touched by his excitement when he first saw water flow from the kitchen faucet. His gestures were unmistakable and soon we all knew when he wanted water, something to eat, or just to go out and play. His sisters were great little teachers and were quite proud of themselves when they quickly got him to say "water," after several repeats.

Ceil followed the suggested menu and prepared chicken and rice. His sisters watched in amazement as he ate the chicken legs and picked the bones clean. He then picked up and ate every piece of rice that fell to the table from his plate. He devoured everything and never wasted a scrap of food. In his own quiet way, he was teaching all of us that food was a precious gift not to be taken for granted. And his healthy appetite always made me smile.

After his twenty-four hour trip from Saigon, he had no trouble falling asleep that first night. We left the lamp on and I slept on the floor alongside his bed. I was glad I did. When the first train went roaring by his window, he sprang up, crying and clawing at the venetian blinds. I wondered if the roar of the train reminded him of the noises of war he'd grown up with. I hugged him and for the first time, he clasped his arms around my neck and slowly relaxed. In no time, he fell back asleep and did not awake again that night as other trains passed. I didn't sleep well after that, wondering what terrible wartime experiences he might have endured in his short life.

Our new son was very fortunate to have three sisters close in age. Between them and his friend, Robby, from next door, he picked up basic English pretty quickly. When words were lacking, he was ingenious in the gestures he would use to communicate. In the beginning, when we went to the Mall, he would stay at Ceil's side, holding her hand. Soon enough, he was off running ahead with his sisters, looking in store windows. He became a part of the family and it was as if he had always been with us.

Although he was raised in a Catholic orphanage in Saigon, we had no record of his baptism. Father Gerry Ryan, of Saint Raymond's, baptized him conditionally and from that day forward, he was James Gerard Verity – "Jimmy" to his family and friends. On the following Sunday, all six of us attended Mass. We remained in the back of the church, close to the exit, in case Jimmy became frightened by the crowds. Father Ryan spotted Jimmy and said he was happy to welcome a new parishioner from Vietnam. He asked me to hold up our son for all to see. When I did so, we were touched as the entire congregation applauded.

Jimmy's color was never an issue with his playmates in early childhood. They played together, shared their toys, and their food. In fact, one of Jimmy's little friends, who had played with him throughout the winter, was amazed one warm spring day when Jimmy took off his sweater to reveal his brown arms. The little boy exclaimed, "Jimmy, your arms are all brown!" After playing together all winter, his little friend never really noticed Jimmy's brown skin – he only saw his friend!

Little children are basically good and tolerant. Bias and prejudice are not part of a child's world. Little Catholic and Protestant children in Ireland can't possibly understand why they throw stones at each other. If we kept the hatred of adults out of the world of Jewish and Palestinian children, they would be laughing and playing together tomorrow. Unfortunately, we adults often fail to do this.

Jimmy and his sister, Eileen, were enrolled in pre-school together. One day, Eileen and another girl were playing together. When Jimmy entered the room to join them, Eileen's companion yelled, "Get out! Black boys can't play in here!" Shocked, Eileen yelled back, "He's my brother. If he can't play, then neither can I!" She then led Jimmy out of the room. If only adults would be so direct when combating racism and demanding tolerance. I always hoped that Eileen might have been more successful in helping to restore the tolerance of her classmate than adults had been in destroying it.

Spending the two full weeks of my summer vacation with Ceil and the kids, was completely refreshing and a total change of pace. On our first family vacation, we traveled to Bar Harbor, Maine, with stops along the way. The major determinant in where we stayed was not the accommodations, but the availability of a swimming pool. The kids couldn't care less if we were in a fancy hotel or a primitive cabin, so long as there was a pool.

When I was a young seminarian, I remember reading about a saint who would jump into a freezing pond to ward off temptations of the flesh. Even then, I thought this was a bit strange and extreme. Little did I ever dream that my day would come when, out of love for my children, I would stand waist deep in Maine pools as each child took turns jumping from the edge of the pool into my arms. Not only did I feel numb from the waist down, but each additional splash of cold water was torture. I was covered in goose bumps! I smiled to myself when I thought of the saint who took a quick dip in freezing water as a sure cure for concupiscence. That was easy. I had no penitential motivation. As a matter of fact, I secretly searched for motel signs that advertised a "Heated Pool." I never found one. What we parents will do for our kids!

The cost of a room and board for six of us became prohibitive. Rather than shorten our vacations, we had to look for an alternative. Throughout Maine, we saw a number of beautiful campgrounds filled with families living in tents, mobile homes, and trailers. The kids were awe struck with the huge swimming pools in a lot of those places.

It wasn't long before Ceil and I spotted a little house trailer for sale. It was a primitive little rust bucket that the six of us could barely squeeze into. Having all of us sleep in it would be tighter than a troop ship but we decided to go for it anyway. The price was right and we were anxious to hit the road. We named our tiny home on wheels, "Benny."

On our very first camping trip, we towed "Benny" into Connecticut. We followed signs down a winding country road to a campground with a pool. After registering for the last vacant site, we entered a campground filled with shiny, silver trailers. It was obviously a convention for seasoned owners of luxurious "Air Stream" trailers. While I nervously tried to maneuver Benny into a tight parking space, I felt as though our refined neighbors must have recalled the movie, "The Grapes of Wrath." In my mind, our arrival must have resembled the scene in which Henry Fonda and his family arrived at a campsite. After the kids got their bathing suits on and made a mad dash for the pool, Ceil and I attempted to relax alongside our trailer. We were well aware that all the neighbors' eyes were upon us. We were slightly uncomfortable, but our childrens' joy and uninhibited laughter was all we needed to feel confident that buying Benny was the right move.

After a few more long trips upstate New York, even as far as Niagara Falls, poor old Benny was ready for the junkyard. We had so much good family fun in Benny that we decided to invest in a bigger, safer trailer, which we named, "Big Ben." While Big Ben had all the conveniences of home, we never brought a radio or a TV on our trips. There was no need. We provided our own entertainment and besides, aside from eating and sleeping, we spent very little time inside.

Life in the campground was simple. The kids practically lived in their bathing suits, which cut down Ceil's trips to the campground laundry. Meals were simple except when Ceil treated us to her famous spaghetti dinners. This was her vacation too, so I took over the outside grill. The kids called me, "Big Mac Jim," famous for cremating burgers. I did a little better with the franks and beans.

Sometimes the aftermath of my franks and beans, could be disastrous. The trailer was about as roomy as a submarine and inevitably, soon after one of these meals, somebody would be screaming, "Pew, it stinks in here!" Usually, one of the kids would also shout, "SBD" – which stood for "silent but deadly." Windows would be cranked opened, fans turned on, and usually the perpetrator could be identified as the one giggling but not complaining. Ceil and I wondered what our neighbors must think about the outbursts, but then again, the Verity clan wasn't the only one in the campground eating franks and beans!

Whether it was Maine or Myrtle Beach, to avoid cabin fever and for a change of pace, we'd leave the campground, go sight seeing, and enjoy a meal out. One such side trip was to the scenic harbor of Camden, Maine. Following a seafood dinner, we all got cones at a local ice cream stand. We no sooner got our cones and started to walk away when our youngest child, Chris, screamed and cried when she lost the scoop of ice cream off her cone. Ceil quieted her, while I got back on line to reorder a replacement cone.

While I was waiting in line, I heard a woman behind me shout, "Holy Shit!" I turned around and there was a nicely dressed, middle aged lady standing on one foot, leaning against her husband with the scoop of Chris' chocolate ice cream mashed between the toes of her sandaled foot. It was an awful mess and I could barely keep a straight face as I carried a fresh cone to Chris. On subsequent trips to Camden, at least one of us recalled the dressy lady with the chocolate foot.

On another day, we took a longer sightseeing trip to Bar Harbor, Maine. Because we would be gone for most of the day, we brought our dog, "Chipper" along with us, rather than leave him alone at the campsite. When we got to Bar Harbor, we parked the wagon under a shady tree, partially opened the windows, and left Chipper in the car. When we returned, the kids panicked. Chipper was gone. I found a note on the dashboard informing us that Chipper was in the police station. My son, Jimmy, accompanied me to the police station. The officer on duty told me that a local "busy body" brought Chipper in. The officer was very nice and said that the dog was in a room down the hall. While we were talking, Jimmy walked down the hall to retrieve Chipper. Once Jimmy returned with the dog, we thanked the officer for being so kind and left the station.

When we got back to car, the girls all hugged Chipper and we left Bar Harbor for the campground. As we got on the open road, Jimmy tapped my shoulder and said, "You know Dad, Chipper pooped all over the floor in the police station." I couldn't believe it! I was so embarrassed that we'd left such a nice cop with such an awful mess. That was our last trip to Bar Harbor!

Big Ben provided us with many years of great trips, but as the children entered high school and got part time jobs, it was time to finally sell the trailer. The new owners, a young couple with six children, would make good use of Big Ben. For any couple that wants to strengthen family ties and enjoy life together, I highly recommend saving your money, buying a tent or trailer, and taking the family camping.

It was during this period, that I joined Saint Raymond's Parish Council and eventually became President. Aside from very routine matters, meetings amounted to little more than rubber-stamping the pastor's suggestions. During my tenure, the most spectacular proposal I made was for the parish to adopt a homeless South Vietnamese family. The immigration services of Catholic Charities informed me that a widowed mother and her four children were in need of a home.

Saint Raymond's owned an under-utilized house and it seemed like an ideal place to care for the Vietnamese family. The pastor, Father Singleton, graciously agreed to open the house to the homeless family. In doing so, he touched the hearts of many parishioners. Word spread quickly. Men, women, and children came forth spontaneously and transformed a partially used house into a comfortable home. Women were scrubbing, cleaning, vacuuming, and hanging curtains. Men were carrying furniture, painting, and transporting supplies. Teens were collecting clothes and toys.

Looking back, I don't know who benefited more from the venture – the parishioners who rallied to help the poor, or the homeless mother and her four children who came to Saint Raymond's with little more than the clothes on their backs. I think it will go down as one of the spiritual highlights in Saint Raymond's parish history. "Whatever you do for the least of my brothers, you do for me."

The fact that our son, Jim, was born in Vietnam made it easy for us to bond with this family. To the mother, Mama Hai, and her children, Ceil and I became known as "Papa Jim" and "Mama Ceil." During the day, Ceil would check on the progress that the new arrivals were making in school. Each night, after work, I would visit them to see how they were adjusting to their new life. On weekends, the five Hais and the six Veritys would pile in our station wagon for trips to the supermarket, beach, or park. We had good times together. But after a year, when the Hais got on their feet, they were ready to join a Vietnamese community in Seattle, Washington. We sadly said our goodbyes and promised to keep each other in our prayers.

When I was actively engaged in the ministry of Saint Gabriel's, I relied heavily on the help of lay volunteers. Many of them were married, full time workers, who relished what little time they could spend with their families. And yet, it seemed the busiest people were always the first to find the time to generously share their talents with those in need. While I was always grateful for their help, I never fully appreciated what I was asking of them. And now, for me as a worker, husband and father, the shoe was on the other foot. It was my turn to volunteer.

Our four children had all done very well in the East Rockaway School District. When I was asked to volunteer to serve as a member of the School Board, I felt I could not refuse. It was payback time. Attending evening board meetings, after a long day at UPS, was no picnic. But my concern for the students kept me motivated. Their well-being was the biggest influence in both my performance on the board and my voting record. Serving on the board was almost like an extension of my youth apostolate on Shelter Island. Differences in times and place didn't change anything – these public school kids were still the hope of our future. Helping them, made the long School Board sessions more than worthwhile.

Because the majority of East Rockaway children attended public school, I was disappointed by the lack of interest the local clergy showed in these young congregants. These youthful members of their parish spent at least 35 hours a week in school but potentially only one hour each week in their houses of worship. The clergy could gain a great deal of insight if they sought first hand information on what transpires in the lives of their youth during school.

During the time I was on the school board, I was surprised to learn of the lack of mutual respect, the prejudice, and the racism existing in the High School. It wasn't all pervasive, but the hate symbols carved into the desks and scratched into the bathroom walls made it painfully obvious that all was not well with some of the young residents in our comfortable little village. A combined effort by the local clergy to promote brotherly love would have done a great deal to help nip this growing prejudice in the bud.

I helped to spear head a committee of very conscientious teachers to promote mutual respect among the student body. I felt strongly that we could not just sit back and do nothing. We needed to open a dialogue with students about issues of race and class. It was too easy for racism to flourish in the tiny, mostly white community. One of my prouder moments on this committee came when I managed to convince the P.T.A. to purchase large reproductions of Norman Rockwell's painting, "Do unto to others as you would have them do to you." This beautiful painting, which to this day still hangs in each of East Rockaway's public schools' lobbies, says a thousand words about mutual respect.

Chapter Thirty-Two

It was at an annual UPS medical exam, that a doctor told me that I needed an aggressive cardiac work-up. He prescribed a Thallium stress test. I guess I shouldn't have been shocked or surprised, especially since there were some isolated episodes that I had ignored and not associated with a heart problem. I always enjoyed good health, having visited an emergency room only once for a sports injury. Now, I found myself being scheduled for periodic visits to a cardiologist, who told me that the symptoms that I had previously ignored, were in fact major warning signs of a serious heart condition.

Leaving UPS was not easy. I had made many good friends on the job. I served the company well and was proud of my attendance record, having missed only one day of work in fifteen years. But the long hours and the daily bumper-to-bumper commute, were slowly and imperceptibly taking their toll on my health. To ignore the warning signs and jeopardize my life, would have been a supreme act of selfishness. Ceil and the children came first. When I returned home from the retirement party, Ceil was waiting for me at the front door. She was all smiles and seemed to read my mind as she hugged me and whispered, "Don't worry about the future. We'll make it." She was right.

Retirement came easy. I had no intention of sitting in a rocking chair, watching the grass grow. It was "catch up time" for home repairs. There was a lot of "Honey, can you do this?" and "Honey, how about that?" There were rooms to be painted, household repairs, etc. Actually, becoming the painter, carpenter, and plumber in our old house was an enjoyable change of pace. After a few months, the interior was finished and I turned my attention to the outdoors. The seasonal changes that Mother Nature provided – the grass, the flowerbeds, the fallen leaves, and the snow, all kept me busy. It was endless and a healthy diversion. I never got bored. I wasn't about to roll over and wait for the undertaker.

I wasn't the only one keeping busy. If keeping busy promotes longevity, Ceil should live to see a hundred. In addition to the non-stop routine of the wife, mother and homemaker, Ceil always managed to stay very involved in childcare. First, she helped out in a local pre-school, then for years she prepared public school children for their First Holy Communion. Later, she was hired by the East Rockaway School District to monitor their lunch program. She was such a hit with the staff and the children, the school eventually asked her to open and direct a "Latch Key" after school program.

The "After School" program was designed to care for the grade school children of working mothers. The program began with a handful of children and steadily grew in proportion to the number of mothers in need of employment. The mothers could relax knowing that their children were in a safe environment. The After School Program ensured mothers that their children would not roam the streets, searching for playmates. Inside the program, were almost a hundred potential playmates. The children were provided with snacks and to the delight of parents, not only was there a playground and organized sports, but there was also a quiet area designated for homework.

Ceil has a special knack for making each child feel important. She knows every child on a first name basis and when one speaks or cries, they get her full attention. She shares their laughter, solves their problems, and dries their tears.

Hardly an evening has gone by, that Ceil hasn't had a humorous story about her After School children. I think what has kept Ceil on the job for seventeen years is the genuine joy she feels upon entering the happy, little world of those innocent children. Jesus once said, "Unless you change and become like children, you will never enter the kingdom of Heaven." Ceil continues to do what she loves and what she does best – she directs the After School program. For her, it is more than a job or a career. Her concern and care for the children borders on a vocation.

Just the other night, she told me about a little boy who confided in her that his first grade classmate did something wrong in the boy's room. After the little informant walked away, she very discreetly asked the accused if anything happened in the boy's room that she needed to know about. The child lowered his little face and with downcast eyes, confessed, "I'm sorry Mrs. Verity, I peed on the floor." Ceil breathed a sigh of relief that it wasn't anything more serious. And she was also certain that the little boy was indeed sorry. So, with a straight face, she said, "Don't do it again. I'll get the custodian to mop it up and so long as you never do it again, I won't tell anyone that this happened." He looked up, smiled, and said, "Okay, I promise." He ran off to join his friends and kept his promise.

I think Ceil's success in the After School program comes from her ability to find some goodness in everyone – to see God's handprint on every child.

Chapter Thirty-Three

After almost thirty years of following a rigid routine, it should have come as no surprise that my biological clock was permanently set to go off at six a.m. Even though I was retired and there was no longer a mad rush to get up and go to work, I was still up at the crack of dawn everyday and ready to go. I guess I'm a morning person. I love the peace and quiet that greets the arrival of each new day.

After putting on the coffee pot and collecting the morning papers off the front lawn, I would catch up on world events. When this quiet time ended, Ceil, like Martha in the scriptures, had a hundred things to do around the house. But being a retiree, I was as free as a bird.

One Friday morning in January of '89, I walked up to Saint Raymond's and caught the 7:30 a.m. Mass. Father John Gilmartin was the celebrant and in his homily he described his work with Catholic Charities. He spoke about the poor, the hungry, and the disabled that Catholic Charities served. At the conclusion of the Mass, I approached him in the sacristy and offered my services as a volunteer for the work of Catholic Charities.

I told Father John about my background as a Passionist priest. He then suddenly recognized me. He remembered a visit that I had made to his home when he was a sixth grade student. I was still active in the priesthood at the time and I visited his home in order to speak to his parents about his brother, Mike, who was considering entering the seminary. Twenty-five years later, the little sixth grader was the director of Catholic Charities. Isn't it mysterious how people from the past keep bobbing to the surface just at the right time?

Without any hesitation, Father John asked me to come to his office in Rockville Centre on Monday morning. I asked John if he wanted more time, reminding him that I would be working in the Chancery building which, was occupied by Bishop McGann and his staff. Although it had been twenty-one years since my departure from the active ministry, there were still members of the clergy who would be uncomfortable in my presence. John did not see this as a problem and encouraged me to come. As it turned out, Bishop McGann was always very kind and friendly. The Bishop recalled the days when, as a Monsignor, he came to Saint Gabriel's for private retreats. Our mutual respect for each other was still intact.

What was most appealing to me about Catholic Charities were the people with whom I associated – both my co-workers and even more so the people we served. This is not to say that Catholic Charities didn't have its share of kings, queens, and drones, like any other human organization. But the vast majority of its people were highly motivated. They were more interested in caring for their less fortunate neighbors than in catering to the more fortunate.

Catholic Charities was an eye opener for me. To read, think, or talk about poverty was one thing, but to come in hand to hand contact with it was a startling experience. To understand hunger, when one has never missed a meal, is almost impossible. It pained me, as a citizen of the richest country in the world, when young mothers and their children came to Catholic Charities because they were undernourished. It saddened me when I saw impoverished seniors slowly inch their way forward on a long line, hoping for handouts of canned goods.

How could I, who was never without a roof over my head, understand homelessness? I had to first meet homeless seniors to even begin to understand their plight. I met one homeless senior who lived in an abandoned car, hidden in a wooded area, not even a mile from the wealthiest estates on Long Island. If it rained, he had to worry about keeping dry. If it snowed, he feared freezing to death. Catholic Charities managed to put this old-timer up in a furnished apartment. He told me that after he awoke from his first night's sleep there, he didn't know if he was dreaming or if he'd died and gone to heaven.

Around December of 1992, I was ordered into Saint Francis Hospital. After staring at the ceiling from a hospital bed and undergoing all kinds of tests for almost a week, it was decided that I needed open heart surgery. On December 7th, a little, retired Sister came into my room and said, "Tomorrow, you're going into the O.R." She said, "It's the feast of the Immaculate Conception. You're in good hands. Mary will watch over you."

The wait for surgery was probably one of the best spiritual retreats I ever made. I never thought I would ever see the day when going to an O.R. was a relief. I was at peace. Ceil and my daughter, Sharon, arrived at Saint Francis at the crack of dawn. They were there to reassure me of their love and prayers, as the gurney rolled into the operating room. Facing surgery and its aftermath, was a lot easier knowing that Ceil and the four kids were praying for me. I was in the hands of both God and the surgeons. Thankfully, all went well and I made a full recovery. Within a very short time, I returned to Catholic Charities.

Once I returned to Catholic Charities, Father John asked me if I would like to be an interfaith pastoral caregiver to the hundreds of residents in our Senior Housing. I jumped at the opportunity. It was something I was not only professionally trained to do, but also something I longed to do. It turned out to be the most rewarding and best possible assignment for me. And to this very day, I remain grateful to Father John.

At this time, there were close to a thousand seniors living in apartments administered by Catholic Charities. Additional sites were in the process of being built, in order to meet the growing need for homes for seniors on low, fixed incomes. Many seniors on Long Island were either unable to maintain their own homes or to afford the apartment rents expected of them. Many of these seniors practiced their faiths their entire lives. They built, supported, and attended their churches, temples, and mosques, and now in their twilight years, they needed more than just a clean, cozy apartment. Catholic Charities' decision to add a spiritual dimension into senior housing, was well received by the residents.

From the very start of my apostolate to seniors of all faiths, I stressed our shared belief in one God. I didn't claim private ownership of God, nor did I argue that my personal path to God was the only one. I was not there to convert or change their approach to God. I was there as a fellow senior who was as much in need of their help in my search for God, as they might have been in need of my help. In time, we learned to share, listen, and trust one another. It was very obvious, from the beginning, that no two seniors were alike. Their personal relationships with God were as unique as their fingerprints. Senior spirituality had its own distinct flavor. It was formed and fashioned by long lives with peaks, valleys, joys, and pains, and it culminated in deep, understanding friendships with God.

In sharing with my seniors, I quickly realized that I had more to learn than to teach – more reason to listen and absorb, than to speak. I definitely had the best assignment Catholic Charities had to offer.

In time, I put together an interfaith prayer card that seniors, of all faiths, found acceptable. Unlike a business card, the prayer card served not only as an introduction, but as a springboard for an explanation of my role as an interfaith pastoral caregiver.

On one occasion, I unknowingly offered the prayer card to a senior who was legally blind. She very graciously accepted it and said, "You know, Jim, I've lost most of my sight. Isn't it strange that even though I can no longer see or even read my prayer book, I can more easily sense God's presence? I can now talk to God, in my own words, and you know – I think God hears me!"

She continued, "It's similar to something I experienced with my husband when he was still alive. The puppy love of our younger days was gone. We would sit together in silence. He never used a book or a poem to describe his love for me. He often didn't even say he loved me and he didn't need to. I just knew he did." She asked if this sounded strange. I said, "I don't think what you just said is strange. I think it's beautiful. In some marvelous way, you communicate with God and by the peacefulness you experience, it's as though God is sitting next to you. In your own words, you just described the presence of

God in your life." This was my first visit, with many more to follow, with my little Presbyterian friend.

Life in a senior apartment can easily become an isolated, lonely existence. The senior's circle of relatives and friends keeps shrinking. The pictures that decorate their walls of spouses, family, and friends are reminders, but not substitutes for those they've loved and lost. They sometimes feel abandoned and alone. They need someone to talk to, to listen to them. They have to be reminded, as was I, that God is as close to them as the air they breathe.

Some seniors have to learn to raise their shades and look out the window once in a while. There's a big, beautiful world out there. God puts on a show every day for us – the beautiful sunrise, the puffy white clouds, and the little bird on the nearby tree. One senior, a former city dweller, who lived most of his life in the concrete jungle, used to rhapsodize to me about the beauty of the roses he raised outside his window. To him, the God whose handiwork was so evident in the beautiful roses, couldn't be far away.

It took a good six months before I was accepted by most seniors. I didn't expect to be greeted with open arms. From day one, I never passed by a resident without a smile and a friendly greeting. I couldn't blame seniors for being cautious, distant, or skeptical. Too often, the elderly were victimized by con artists. I was a new comer on the scene and gradually they would compare notes, sound me out, and make their own decisions about me. Little by little, the walls began to crumble. We were getting to know each other on a first name basis. When visiting sites, I made it a practice to first drop into the laundry room. This was a great gathering place. Someone was always doing a wash or waiting for the dryer. It was a place for casual introductions and for making small talk.

It was early one morning when I began a sixty mile drive from my home to a senior residence in Hampton Bays. It was a cold, dreary morning. The closer I got to the east end of Long Island, the more the rain turned from a light drizzle into a freezing rain. When I drove into the residence, not a senior could be found. Seniors fear slippery sidewalks.

I went directly to the laundry and sure enough, there was one lonely senior doing a wash. I had never met her before and didn't know her name. She had an idea of who I was from reading my monthly bulletin. I introduced myself and asked how she was. She answered, "I'm alright but I'm worried about my son who is seriously ill in Stonybrook Hospital." I told her that I was a priest and served as a hospital chaplain many times. When I offered to visit her son, her face lit up. She was all smiles but expressed her concern about the reception he might give me. I told her that I would call her after my visit with him.

No other seniors were in sight, so I took off for Stonybrook Hospital. The driving conditions worsened and I was tempted to delay the visit for another day. The fact that I drove sixty miles to see only this one, sole senior, who was terribly worried about the spiritual welfare of her dying son, was no coincidence. It was meant to be. I was sure that God had His hand in this, and so, I set off for the hospital.

When I entered the man's room, I knew his mother's prayers were heard. He welcomed me. We prayed together and he asked for absolution. He was at peace.

When I spoke to his mother later, she informed me that her son had died. She was at peace as a mother and I, as a priest, could not help but think that God had arranged the whole thing. He wanted me to be in the right place, at the right time!

I do not want to mislead anyone or give the impression that I was the long awaited Messiah or the pied piper that seniors flocked to. Senior housing had its share of lonely, disgruntled, grumpy old people. But, they were in the minority. Some eventually came around, said, "Hello," smiled, and, miracles of miracles, even joined our group activities!

On my morning visits, I would regularly cross paths with a frail, gruff old man who often muttered little digs at me, or totally ignored me. His behavior intrigued me. I didn't know if he was testing me, looking for an argument, or just trying to scare me off. This went on for some time. Then, he suddenly disappeared and I realized that I missed our little encounters.

I was told that he was bed ridden, in a lot of pain, and unable to leave his apartment. I was also informed that, from his youth, he had spent a lot of time in hospitals. Poor man, he probably experienced more pain in one week than I had in a lifetime. Pain was his constant companion.

I decided to start making regular visits to his apartment. During these visits, we had many discussions about God and the Catholic Church. He loved to bait me, to get under my skin. Our relationship gradually improved, to the point where I could call him a "stubborn old coot," which seemed to please him. He never told me who or what caused him to leave the church. But even through his negativity, something powerful shined through that convinced me that his faith in God was still alive. Of course, he'd be the last to admit this.

I was with him the last time he was readmitted to the hospital. Before leaving his bedside, I told him that I would pray for him only if he would pray for me. He looked me in the eyes, smiled, and nodded his head in agreement. I think this was the only time I ever saw the old coot let his guard down.

Two days later, as I was driving down the expressway, I got a call from an undertaker who informed me that my old friend had passed and had requested that I conduct his funeral service. In the presence of four mourners, I eulogized my argumentative friend who reminded me of the repentant thief on Calvary. In his dying moments, my old friend, too, was consoled by Jesus' promise of his place in paradise. In the eyes of human beings, this man may have appeared irreligious. In the eyes of God, this was a man who for most of his life, hung on his own cross of pain. I'm sure he, too, had the ear of his redeemer who welcomed him into paradise that day.

I always felt extremely blessed to be able to associate daily with so many wonderful seniors. There was diminutive Esther, a little Jewish lady, who seemed to have jumped right out of the Old Testament. She was the epitome of hospitality with a generous heart, that must have been half the size of her body. She was never happier than when I would accept her invitation to share a bowl of her famous turkey soup. In the same housing complex, there was a man who was physically disabled from birth, but never missed an opportunity to get out of his room. Every bus ride he took to Church or the supermarket was a physical challenge, but he met that challenge whenever it was presented. His determination was inspiring.

At another site, there were two men, Ed and Fred, both with razor sharp minds. They were great conversationalists with incredible stories to share. Ed, a World War II vet, who received the Silver Star and was disabled, never let his disability prevent him from volunteering his services at a hospital each week. I could always count on Ed to be the spark plug who would liven up my group discussions.

In our monthly discussion groups, we had a complete cross-section of humanity – Protestants, Jews, Muslims, Catholics, and non-believers. In these rap sessions, I would introduce some general spiritual topic as a springboard for discussion. Some seniors were shy and hesitant to share their personal beliefs. It usually took one brave soul to get things started. One of my favorite seniors was a jovial Baptist, originally from the south. She was so comfortable in her beliefs and in God's presence that you would think she was sitting on God's lap. For her, God was no abstract deity, but her heavenly Father and daily companion.

During one of our discussions, a young lady approached me and asked me to visit her sick mother. Her mother was a very active senior and very respected by her neighbors. Her mother often spoke proudly of her son, who was preparing for the Lutheran ministry. When I entered the elderly woman's apartment, she was surrounded by her family. I was shocked by her greeting. She looked up at me and simply said, "Jim, I'm going to die soon. When I go to heaven, I'm going to ask God to bless you and your bishop for taking such good care of us seniors." I joined her and her family in reciting our favorite senior prayer. She was happy and gave me a hug before I left. I was incredibly touched and inspired.

A short time later, I attended her funeral at Holy Redeemer Lutheran Church. The church was filled with family, friends, and admirers. I had the privilege of knowing this great lady who taught all of us how to be happy with God in both life and death.

There was nothing heroic about my ministry to the elderly. I was well rewarded for my feeble efforts. The people I served were amazing. They taught me how to live and how to die. For example, I visited an elderly lady in hospice. She was well aware that she was dying. When I entered the room, her husband was sitting at her bedside. No words were being spoken as they held hands. It was a private, sacred time and I feared that I was intruding. As I backed out of the room, she opened her eyes, smiled, and said, "Oh Jim, how good of you to visit!" All I could say was, "You are the good one. You have always been so good and kind and God loves you for it." I offered my blessing and quickly left – leaving these two, devoted lovers alone for the little time they had left together.

A few years ago, I visited an infirmary for elderly Sisters who spent their religious lives caring for others. About a half mile away, was a priest who had the reputation of being a great golfer. Walking eighteen holes was no great challenge for him. But walking a short distance to the infirmary to offer Mass for the elderly Sisters, was not among his priorities. I found this painful. Once again, I, having received all seven sacraments, asked myself if it was right for me to submerge the sacrament of Holy Orders and deprive the Sisters of the priestly ministry they deserved.

A short time ago, a priest said to me, "It must be very painful for you to not say Mass." If he meant donning the vestments for my personal satisfaction, I would have to answer, "No, it is not painful for me to participate in a Mass celebrated by another." I never looked upon the priesthood as a private source of spiritual joy. Any joy that comes from the priesthood, should flow from the service to others.

As far as I'm concerned, Holy Orders is an active sacrament. For me, the priesthood has never really been dormant, but mysteriously seems to surface quietly at the precise time when someone is in need of it. Although I have never offered Mass or publicly officiated as a priest since laicization, I cannot count the number of times on the highway, at work, or in the elderly homes that the hidden priesthood surfaces. For the benefit of the dying, it seemed I was often in the right place, at the right time. It was meant to be.

Chapter Thirty-Four

In September 2000, as I walked across the parking lot at Mercy Hospital, on my way to visit an elderly patient, I felt an old, familiar warning sign in my chest. It wasn't terribly painful but it was the type of pain that my cardiologist warned me not to ignore. At this point, I knew how important it was to listen to the messages my body sends.

Before visiting a patient, I always dropped into the hospital chapel to ask God to bless the sick. On this day, I asked God for a quick injection of prudence so that I could weigh all the options and make the right decision about the future. Do I resign from Catholic Charities and end my ministry to the seniors or do I push the envelope and hope for the best? Something Oscar Romero, the bishop of San Salvador once said came to mind, "We are ministers, not messiahs." I was not indispensable; certainly there were others who could minister to the seniors.

On the other hand, there was no one to replace me as a husband and father. There was just too much love between Ceil, the children, and I to find a substitute. The decision came quickly. As I left the chapel, I knew my ten years at Catholic Charities had come to an end.

I would miss my co-workers for their friendship and the inspiration they gave me in their service to their less fortunate brothers and sisters. But I would mostly miss those who opened up a whole new world of senior spirituality, those wonderful old women and men who taught me powerful lessons about the love of God and neighbor. With them, I learned to walk the walk, instead of just talking the talk. I love them all.

2001 and 2002 were such busy years. They really flew by. From the time I rolled out of bed at the crack of dawn, until the time I conked out at night in front of the TV, I was active. Life seemed to be on the fast track.

I think one of the greatest blessings of my retirement is the precious, relaxed morning time that I am able to spend with my wife, Ceil. For thirty years, I began the day rushing around the house, getting ready for work, and then jumping into the car to follow a long line of taillights into work. I didn't know what I had been missing. And now, Ceil and I are two empty-nesters enjoying our coffee, reading the papers, and chatting about our children.

But our peaceful routine was shattered on that September morning when Ceil and I watched the unbelievable sight of one plane, and then a second, rip into the World Trade Center. Then, a third plane plunged into the Pentagon and a fourth crashed into a Pennsylvania field. These incomprehensible acts of evil left us speechless. It was all so sudden and terrible.

Right in the middle of all this horror, our phone rang. It was our daughter, Sharon. She was at work in Brooklyn and wanted to let us know that she was safe. Her subway passed under the World Trade Center a half hour before the first plane hit. Our youngest, Chris, called from Manhattan saying she couldn't get to work but was very concerned about a friend who worked in the Twin Towers. She later learned that her friend had perished with so many others. Eileen from Boston and Jimmy from Rochester, both called to check on the safety of their two sisters. Later in the day, Sharon called to tell us that she was leaving work and was going to try to volunteer in the emergency room of the Beekman Downtown hospital. For the remainder of the day, our prayers were bouncing back and forth between thanking God for the safety of our children and praying for the thousands of victims and their loved ones.

Seeing the lifeless body of Fire Chaplain, Father Judge, being carried from the fallen tower made me very sad, but at the same time, very proud of this heroic priest who died while ministering to the fallen firemen. As reports came in about the hundreds of firemen who perished, I thought of my father's old company, Rescue # 4. I was certain that some its brave men would be among the victims. I was saddened and, in some small way, could empathize with the wives and children who were most certainly hoping and praying their firemen would return safely home.

With each passing day, the ripple effect kept widening – relatives, friends, cops, firemen, office workers, and neighbors were missing. For an entire year, the mournful tolling of church bells and the sound of bag pipes could be heard as friends and relatives gathered to grieve for those who had perished.

Only our faith and trust in God could help us cope with such indescribable evil. The threat of terrorists secretly operating in our midst can easily paralyze us with a haunting fear. My family and I discussed the importance of being able to place ourselves in the protective palms of God's hands.

One morning in March 2002, Sharon and I took Ceil to Saint Francis Hospital for what we thought would be a routine check-up and a quick return home. After examining Ceil, Dr. Pappas, our cardiologist, asked Sharon and me to follow him to Ceil's bedside. There, he described her condition and recommended immediate by-pass surgery. In less than an hour, Ceil was on her way to the operating room. It was shocking and frightening. We relayed the news to Eileen, Chris, and Jimmy, all of whom immediately traveled to Saint Francis.

Keeping vigil for Ceil while she was in surgery was far more stressful than anything I had experienced ten years earlier during my own by-pass. For the anesthetized patient, the operating room almost feels like a suspension of life – there are no worries, no stress, no pain, and no sense of time. In the waiting room, time seems to stand still and the anxiety is unbearable. The minutes drag by and the only relief available comes from praying and leaning on loved ones.

By the time Ceil was regaining consciousness, the five of us were all at her bedside. I can't imagine going through such radical surgery and then opening one's eyes to an empty room. Family love has a way of sharing pain, shattering loneliness, and speeding up recovery.

Before long, Ceil and I began our daily morning walks along the boardwalk of Long Beach. What a joy to walk hand in hand with Ceil and to see her strength gradually return. Six months later, a team of ten horses couldn't have kept Ceil away from her Latch-Key program and the children. She survived and was ready to re-embrace life. It was meant to be – God has her in the palm of His hand.

Chapter Thirty-Five

By 2002, as the impact of September 11th, was slowly moving off the front pages, the media began to focus on another structure threatening to collapse from within. The media was cashing in on the sex scandals in the Catholic Church. News reports about pedophile priests began in Boston and quickly spread like wild fire in other dioceses across the country. The scandal was out in the open. There were no more secrets. Local victims were making accusations, neighborhood priests were being arrested, and local bishops were accused of cover-ups. The laity was shocked, confused, and disillusioned. The scandals became a daily topic of discussion on the job, the street, and at the supper table. And while the media had a lot to say about the scandal, the diocesan papers said little and the pulpits were, for the most part, silent on the subject.

When I remember the horror that I experienced as a boy trapped in the woods with a pedophile, I shudder to think of the fear that a child being sexually abused by a clergyman experiences. Priests are placed on a pedestal for supposedly leading virtuous lives. Who can these betrayed children turn to for help? Where does a child find the words to describe the experience? Would the accusation made by the child be taken seriously or brushed aside? And if the child's report was taken seriously, what would the follow-up be? Would the sinful clergyman be summoned by his superior and simply scolded, transferred, and told to sin no more? Judging from the horror stories of pedophilia in the media, more often than not, the victim was scarred for life while the predator was spared. Bishops, more concerned about the reputation of the institutional church, were soothed by the belief that a major scandal was squelched.

During this time of scandal, I had many discussions with my wife around the kitchen table and with my daughters over the phone. Eileen, the social worker in Boston, witnessed the anger and protests of the laity, not only because of the sins of the priest but also because of the cover-ups within the hierarchy. Sharon, the physician assistant, was concerned that not enough attention was being paid to the abused children and how to help them heal. Christine, the lawyer, was saddened and distressed at the manner in which all priests were finding themselves under a cloud of suspicion. She was also disturbed at the hierarchy's handling of the situation. They had ignored the problem for so long and now were casting priests out, without so much as a trial, in order to distance themselves from any culpability. This was certainly true of the bishop who referred to an accused priest as a "contract worker." If this remark upset me, I can only imagine what the conversation was like around the rectory supper tables that night!

About fifteen years ago, when I was conducting religious education classes in my home, I invited a parish priest into my home as a guest teacher for one class. He gave an inspirational talk and offered Mass for the class. He impressed all of us as a holy priest and learned teacher. Recently, that same priest was accused of sexually assaulting a child. He was arrested, proven guilty in a court of law, and sent to prison. In the eyes of the Church, he committed a serious sin. In the eyes of the State, he committed a serious crime, punishable by a prison sentence.

In my eyes and in the eyes of my children, who helped me welcome him into our home, the immediate reactions were shock and sadness. Shock because he had never given any indication of any deviant behavior. On the contrary, he always seemed like such a good priest. Sadness because the one evil act he committed will overshadow and blot out all the good that he had done over the years. As a parent, I grieve for the little boy, the victim scarred for life with a terrible memory. As a parent, I can also understand the anger towards the priest who victimized a child. As a fellow priest, I cannot understand or condone what he did. However, I also leave it up to God to judge. I certainly don't want to be numbered among the hypocrites, like those in the gospel, who were about to condemn the sinful woman when Jesus rebuked them, "Let he who is without sin throw the first stone."

The catechism of the Catholic Church says, "The whole church is a priestly people. This participation through baptism is called the 'common priesthood of the faithful.'" The catechisms go on to say that lay people have the right and at times, even the duty, to express their opinions on matters that pertain to the good of the church.

And yet in some dioceses, the doors of the parish building have been ordered closed to the lay people who want to voice their opinions on matters which they feel pertain to the good of the church. A business in the private sector wouldn't last very long if the C.E.O. locked his office door to avoid facing objective criticism from his staff and customers. How can a bishop not be aware of the decline in attendance at Sunday Mass, the decrease in collections, and the scathing criticism in the media? Promising future meetings with selective audiences is not the answer for the troubled faithful. A bishop who has ears only for praise and good news, is like a parent who rejoices in the laughter of his child but can't hear the cries.

There was a time when priests would have jovial reunions with classmates to celebrate the anniversaries of their ordinations. There were diocesan meetings scheduled by the bishops for all priests to attend. At the diocesan meetings, the priests, almost like frightened business men in front of their C.E.O.'s, would remain quiet and submissive when they were addressed. Today, thankfully, a new and courageous priesthood is emerging. Good, holy, dedicated priests are working hard in the vineyard of the Lord. They are signing petitions, speaking out, and demanding to be heard. These priests are saddened and embarrassed, not only by the misconduct of their peers, but also by the behavior of their leaders – leaders who attempt to deflect public scrutiny by distancing themselves from any personal blame in the mishandling of scandals.

I feel sorry for the priests who have to second guess everything they do with young parishioners. They have to fear that well intentioned and pure acts might be misinterpreted. It's open season on the clergy. One false accusation of a serious nature can destroy a good reputation, activate a vicious rumor mill, and destroy the zeal of a dedicated priest. If there was ever a time that priests needed the support of their leaders, it is now.

Never in my lifetime have I seen the priesthood, of which I will always be proud to share, take such serious hits. Now, more than ever, it is time for priests to walk tall, wear the collar, and emulate Christ. The laity is confused and hurt. And in this time of serious crisis, Rome is not sending clear messages. Rome continues to tell us when to stand and sit during Mass. Eucharistic ministers, without any plausible explanation, are told they may distribute Holy Communion, but may not cleanse the sacred vessels. This is like telling someone that it's okay to pass out the food but it's forbidden to wash the dishes.

On Sunday mornings, I notice many of my fellow parishioners checking their watches when a certain priest comes rushing into the sanctuary, at the very last minute, to set up the altar for Mass. He keeps hundreds of parishioners waiting but never apologizes or offers an explanation for his tardiness. This same priest always tells the congregation to remain for the full liturgy and not to leave early. Doesn't he realize that if he started Mass on time, he would not only finish on time but would have a lot more parishioners around after Mass to shake his hand? Arrogance has no place in the priesthood.

I personally know a man in his mid-eighties who attended Sunday Mass faithfully for his entire life. Every week, he generously filled the collection basket with all he could afford. Each year, he managed to scrape together a thousand dollars for the Bishop's Appeal. This parishioner has been in a nursing home for the past two years. His life savings has been completely diminished. He is now on Medicaid. The collection envelopes still come to his old address but no priest has ever come to his new address – the nursing home - to visit him!

In these financially difficult times for the church, the new bishop of Boston put the Episcopal mansion up for sale and opted to share an apartment with his priests. That is admirable.

In another diocese, the new bishop furnishes a new mansion and moves out of the priest residence. Again, there is a mixed message and the laity is confused.

When collection baskets are over-flowing, it is easy to preach about the preferential option for the poor. But when the collections decline, the first parishioners to feel the pinch are the poor. How can anyone in the diocese, with a full stomach, even think about closing a food pantry? When the thermometer drops below freezing, the congregation will generously contribute to the fuel bill. Why should the warmth of parish facilities not be shared with the homeless? The Church needs to remind itself of the scene in Bethlehem, when a young, homeless couple seeking shelter had doors closed in their faces. Who decides that God's house is no longer a haven of hospitality?

At the height of the sexual scandal, Father John Geoghan, the predator priest in Boston, received so much coverage in the media that I felt like I knew him. When he was finally sent to prison, I think the hierarchy and many priests, all breathed a sigh of relief. It was a case of "out of sight, out of mind."

Then, Father Geoghan was brutally murdered in prison and deprived of his right to life. In a television interview, a Catholic layman commented, "Geoghan got what he deserved!" Bishops, who led "Right to Life" marches, and priests, who spoke eloquently from the pulpit against capital punishment, were suddenly silent about the murder of this unpopular priest.

Such a powerful homily could have been given on the occasion of this imprisoned priest's murder. The repentant thief, who hung on a cross alongside of Christ, asked forgiveness for a lifetime of sin. The sins of the thief were no match for the mercy of Jesus, who assured him of his place in paradise. Geoghan's crimes were heinous and sinful. But all of us, sinners and saints, have a right to life. All sinners are in need of God's mercy – there can be no exceptions. Life is too precious. It is a gift from God and only God should give it and take it away. I waited, week after week, for a homily that touched on these points. Such a homily never came and I asked myself, "Why the silence?"

Although disappointed about the silence surrounding Geoghan's murder, I am also well aware of the incredible efforts made by the vast majority of priests. One Sunday morning, a few weeks ago, Ceil and I stood in Mass, as the cross bearer, altar girls, Eucharistic ministers, and finally the celebrant processed up the center aisle of the Church. We whispered in agreement that the priest looked drawn and exhausted. Later, during the Mass, the priest mentioned that he was substituting for his colleague who was sick. He mentioned that he, too, had been sick during the week. He then posed a rhetorical question, "To whom would you turn, if we were both sick at the same time?"

Thousands of good priests across the country are tired, sickly, and being pushed to the limit. Some are bordering on complete exhaustion. These priests, with no relief in the foreseeable future, must ask themselves "Who will minister to my flock when I am no longer able?"

I know my answer to that question. I am ready, willing, and able to resume the ministry. Looking around at the laity that morning, I wondered what their answers would be. I also wondered what their reaction to my answer would be.

Another thing jumped to my attention that morning. When I looked at the sanctuary, I realized that the priest was surrounded by all women – the Eucharistic ministers, the lector, and all the altar servers were females. Isn't it strange that, until quite recently, only men were seen in the sanctuary? Is the presence of women in the sanctuary and in administrative positions in the diocese a trend that might eventually lead to the ordination of women? The answer is no, according to a recent pronouncement from the Holy See. The possibility of women being ordained is apparently even less plausible than allowing a married priest to function in the ministerial priesthood. And yet, there are no clear reasons for these pronouncements.

Is there something in the past two thousand years that has proven that only men are capable of administering the sacraments? Even though Mary and the women of the scriptures are not mentioned as having actively participated in the Last

Supper, they were probably present, preparing food and reverently observing Jesus and the apostles from the kitchen door. On Good Friday, with the exception of one apostle, it was Mary, the mother of Jesus, and the women of Jerusalem who stood at the foot of the cross. No human shared more intimately in the sacrifice of Jesus than his mother, who fashioned his flesh and blood, and gave him the life he willingly sacrificed.

I wonder, given the choice, would the saintly Mother Teresa have chosen to be canonized a saint in death or ordained a priest in life so that she could administer the Sacrament of the Sick to the poor in Calcutta? Which would she have chosen? What do you think?

Chapter Thirty-Six

John the Baptist was such a holy man and fiery preacher that people sometimes confused him for the Messiah they were awaiting. John, who was famous for his straight forward nature, told the crowds that he was not the Messiah but that they should prepare for his arrival. John's uncensored preaching got him into trouble with those who had no intention of changing their lifestyles. He was imprisoned for disturbing the consciences of the unrepentant and was unjustly beheaded.

While in prison, John heard about Christ's activities and sent his disciples to Jesus to ask him if he was the Messiah or if he needed to wait for another. Jesus answered, "Go back and tell John about what you are hearing and seeing. The blind can see, the lame can walk, lepers are cured, the deaf hear, the dead are brought back to life, and the poor have the good news preached to them. Happy are those that have no doubts about me!"

Judging from the comments I hear and from the increasing number of empty pews in Mass each week, I feel the laity is now paraphrasing John the Baptist's question to Jesus, "Is this the right Church or should we be looking for another?" The image of the Church has been tarnished. Church members are disenchanted. For many, the Church seems to be on a razor's edge – has it bottomed out or will it plunge even farther? Will it recover and grow stronger than ever? Is this the true Church or do I look for another?

Have you ever experienced a time in your own life when you were in need of encouragement or inspiration and a Christ-like person came along to intensify your faith in God, your hope for the future, and your love of God and neighbor? I know I have. I didn't have to ask if I was in the right place, at the right time. I knew I was.

When the Holy See was becoming stuffy, bureaucratic, and complacent, it was John XXIII who threw open the windows and breathed new life into the Church by convening the Second Vatican Council. This down to earth, humble shepherd would leave the comfort of the Vatican to visit prisoners in the city jails and the poor in the slums of Rome. He set a wonderful example for the Church leadership.

Pope John also had a sense of humor. A story was told about a visitor to the Vatican who was overwhelmed by the number of Cardinals, Bishops, priests, and laymen he saw running around with attaché cases and files. He asked the Pope, "How many people work here?" Pope John smiled and answered, "About half of them." When the Holy See seemed aloof and out of touch with the ordinary churchgoer, it was John, the peoples' Pope, who gave us a sense of belonging. He was truly a Holy Father.

When Oscar Romero was promoted to Archbishop of San Salvador, he was courted by the elite and the powerful of a corrupt government. His acceptance of gifts or willingness to socialize would have been interpreted as his stamp of approval. Archbishop Romero's options were very similar to those of John the Baptist. He could choose to be quiet and not rock the boat; he could take the path of least resistance and lead a comfortable life. The other option was to struggle for a peace that comes from giving to the poor, the sick, and the downtrodden – seeking justice for all. To denounce the violent oppression, was to incur the wrath of the oppressors. John the Baptist was beheaded for defending the sanctity of marriage. Oscar Romero was assassinated while celebrating Mass, as punishment for his defense of the poor.

Women have also been a source of great inspiration for me, particularly women who were devoted in their service to the poor. American women ministered to the poor in Central America and were murdered in the process. Dorothy Day devoted her long, and at times, tempestuous life to caring for the poor in the slums of the United States. Dorothy Day didn't mince words. She was outspoken and got right to the heart of the matter.

"I wanted the churches to open their doors, to let the poor and the hungry and the homeless come inside, to feed them, to give them shelter. I wanted all the gold and the furs, all the fancy jewels worn by the princes of the church, the prelates – all that to be sold, so men and women and children could get a meal and not shiver and get sick on the streets with no place to go." - Dorothy Day

Dorothy Day was fearless in the face of criticism and opposition from the highest quarters. And she did more than just "talk the talk." To this day, the doors of her "Houses of Hospitality" are wide open to the homeless and the poor.

Not too long ago, a holy man famous for speaking the truth, Cardinal Joseph Bernardin of Chicago, was falsely accused of sexual misconduct. This false accusation was more painful and disturbing to him than the terminal cancer that was consuming his body. The Cardinal clung to the truth and continued to profess his innocence until the false charges were eventually retracted. His love for the truth was matched only by the forgiveness and compassion he showed to the man who falsely accused him.

"My first worry was about the impact that these imputations of my character would have on the church.

The attack was directed against the most important thing I had going for me as a religious leader – my reputation. If my credibility was destroyed, so was my ability to lead." Cardinal Joseph Bernardin

A few years ago, while I was still at Catholic Charities, I traveled to a poor section of Long Island in order to inform the local clergy, of all faiths, that a new housing complex was available to low income seniors. During a visit to a very poor Episcopal Church, the pastor and I struck up a conversation. After I informed him that I was formerly an active Catholic priest, he told me about a Catholic priest who was now a pastor of an Episcopal parish. He said this priest was very successful. In the course of the conversation, this Episcopal priest expressed that he couldn't understand Rome's hard line against optional celibacy when the laity were suffering from the priest shortage. He then suggested that I activate my ministerial priesthood in the Episcopal Church. This suggestion from a good and holy man was very tempting. It suddenly became my turn to ask, "Is the Catholic Church the Church I want or should I look for another?"

As a laymen and a priest, I have devoted my entire life to the Catholic Church. It has not been a one-way street. During the course of my lifetime, I have met and been deeply influenced by spiritual giants in the religious life, the priesthood, and among the laity. I've inherited a spiritual legacy from people like Pope John XXIII, Oscar Romero, Dorothy Day, Joseph Bernardin, and church members who shall remain nameless. These holy, courageous people who have walked the earth with me, are now enjoying their rewards in heaven. But I take refuge in the thought that new, holy, Christ-like leaders will emerge to restore the Church and encourage the rest of us in our attempts to imitate Christ.

As a teenager in the minor seminary, I often thought that it would have been easier to become holy if I had lived during the time of Christ. How inspiring it would have been to listen to Jesus on the hillside and at the seashore! What an incentive it would have been to imitate his kindness to children, his caring for the poor and the hungry. These were the dreams of a teenager looking for an easier way to be Christ-like. But this just wasn't meant to be.

And now, two thousand years after Christ, I live in a very different world where much has changed. But Jesus' message hasn't changed – his challenge to love God and my neighbor remains. Human nature also hasn't changed. My mind has been designed to search for the truth, my will yearns for what is good, and God is always ready to help me in both pursuits. And during my lifetime, I have shared my days with the same kind of courageous men and women who stepped out of the crowd to follow Christ.

2002 has been a trying time for the Church and for all of us. There has been a lot head shaking and finger pointing. It's time to turn the fingers around and do some self-examination. It's time for a renewal of spirit, a personal and humble imitation of Christ.

The challenge of being a good Christian spans a lifetime. It never ends and yet the challenge constantly changes. It changes from day to day, hour to hour, and even minute to minute. Being Christ-like can only take place in the present, depending on the circumstances in which I find myself – at home, in the mall, with friends or strangers, or in a traffic jam. It's easy to appear Christ-like in the peaceful atmosphere of a Church. The real challenge is remaining Christ-like on the other side of those Church doors.

There are two things that never change in the imitation of Christ. Jesus warned us about one, "If a man wishes to come after me, he must deny himself, take up his cross, and follow in my steps." The crowds that followed Jesus on Palm Sunday thinned out drastically when the cross came into sight on Good Friday. If following Jesus was easy, we would have a lot more company in our attempts to be Christ-like.

The second unchanging characteristic is to remain aware of Christ's constant presence in our lives. Remember the words of Isaiah the prophet, "See, I will not forget you. I have carved you in the palm of my hand." And at the Last Supper, Jesus promised His apostles, "I will not leave you orphans." While totally respecting our free will, God, in some mysterious and marvelous way, still manages to remain present in our lives and nudges us to model our behavior after Christ's. These moments don't need to be anything spectacular. It could be as simple as a seemingly chance meeting with a very inspirational person. It might happen when meeting a group of oppressed people, desperately in need of our help. Or perhaps it might happen with the disturbing realization that one's own life is in shambles and needs renewal.

The terrorism of 2001 and the Church sex scandal of 2002, demonstrated how a comparatively small number of people can inflict great harm on so many others. The rippling effects of their evil acts continue to affect us as we enter 2003. Is it too far fetched to think that 2003 could be the beginning of our renewal, a time for healing? The goodness and the holiness of even the most unnoticed people, have an intangible, but effective way of radiating Christ and counteracting evil. Nothing discourages the performance of evil more than the silent rebuke that comes from the presence of holiness.

> *"We cannot do everything, and there is a sense of liberation in realizing that. This enables us to do something, and to do it very well. It may be incomplete, but it is a beginning, a step along the way, an opportunity for the Lord's grace to enter and do the rest." – Oscar Romero*

Chapter Thirty-Seven

Ceil and I may be what people refer to as "Empty Nesters," but not a day goes by that we don't talk about or communicate with our four children. If it isn't phone calls, it's emails. Every morning, Sharon, the physician assistant, calls us during her commute to Saint Raphael's emergency room. Eileen, the full time social worker and part time law student, usually calls us from Boston in the evening. Christine, who is practicing law in New Orleans, calls everyday and fills us in on the preparations she is making for her upcoming marriage to Dr. Ricardo Monserrate on July 26, 2003.

My son, Jim, and I, are not natural phone people. A few sentences suffice and then we usually turn the phone over to the ladies, who never seem lost for words. But Jim has his own way of communication. At the end of a visit he made with his wife and two children, I found a little note that Jim had attached to my growing manuscript. He wrote, "Hey Dad, if you're ever lost for words, write down how much your kids love you and

Mom." We are a very close family. If the phone ever stopped ringing, I would quickly begin to worry.

Ceil and I still make our daily, early morning trips to Long Beach for our strolls on the boardwalk. After our hand in hand walks, we usually find an empty bench and sit mesmerized by the show that God and Mother Nature put on for us. No two mornings are ever quite the same. The colors of the sky vary. There are white puffy clouds some days, dark, menacing ones on others. One morning the surf is rough, the next day calm. Sometimes, the sea gulls, gliding overhead, catch my eye. Other days, the little sand pipers, running along the water's edge, are what capture my attention. All of this takes place with the broad expanse of the ocean and the distant horizon as a backdrop – a big picture which creates a very calming and peaceful atmosphere.

With Ceil alongside me and the Creator's handiwork surrounding us, it is easy to sense God's presence. There is never a hint of loneliness. In such a setting, I can only thank God for Ceil, my children, and all the good people in my life. The peace and happiness that has been a part of my life is not the result of human effort alone, nor is it the product of pure chance. God has always had me in the palm of His hand.

And so for the future, we have to keep our ears open to hear the whispers of God. We have to keep our eyes focused to recognize God in the faces of those around us. And we have to keep our shoelaces tied and be ready to move in any direction that God points out to us.

About twenty years ago, Pope John Paul II reminded one of his assistants in Rome, "Don't ever forget that there are no coincidences. It's all in God's providence and in God's design."

Ceil puts it more simply, "IT WAS MEANT TO BE."

Epilogue

James Gerard Verity

October 14, 1925 – March 30, 2004

James Gerard Verity passed away approximately one month after completing his memoir. Jim spent his entire life giving and continues to give, even after death. These words were his final gift to us. We will forever treasure them, along with our memories and love for him. Like their author, these words are inspiring and filled with compassion and wisdom. And so, in honor of Jim's spirit, we wanted to share them with you.

The Verity Family

Printed in the United States
26461LVS00003B/160-183

9 781420 828443